Jewish
Philosophy as
a Guide to Life

THE HELEN AND MARTIN SCHWARTZ LECTURES IN JEWISH STUDIES

Sponsored by the
Robert A. and Sandra S. Borns
Jewish Studies Program
Indiana University

Jewish Philosophy as a Guide to Life

Rosenzweig, Buber, Levinas, Wittgenstein

Hilary Putnam

Indiana University Press

BLOOMINGTON AND INDIANAPOLIS

This book is a publication of

Indiana University Press
601 North Morton Street
Bloomington, IN 47404-3797 USA

http://iupress.indiana.edu

Telephone orders   800-842-6796
Fax orders   812-855-7931
Orders by e-mail   iuporder@indiana.edu

The paper used in this publication meets the minimum requirements of American National Standard for Information Sciences—Permanence of Paper for Printed Library Materials, ANSI Z39.48-1984.

Manufactured in the United States of America

Library of Congress Cataloging-in-Publication Data

Putnam, Hilary.
   Jewish philosophy as a guide to life : Rosenzweig, Buber, Levinas, Wittgenstein / Hilary Putnam.
      p. cm. — (The Helen and Martin Schwartz lectures in Jewish studies)
   ISBN-13: 978-0-253-35133-3 (cloth : alk. paper)
   1. Philosophy, Jewish. 2. Judaism. 3. Rosenzweig, Franz, 1886–1929. 4. Buber, Martin, 1878–1965. 5. Lévinas, Emmanuel. 6. Wittgenstein, Ludwig, 1889–1951. I. Title.
   B755.P88 2008
   181'.06—dc22

                                                                                    2007043966

1 2 3 4 5   13 12 11 10 09 08

For Ben-Zion Gold
with gratitude and affection

Contents

Preface

The essays that make up this volume grew out of the invitation to give the Helen and Martin Schwartz Lectures on Jewish Studies at Indiana University in 1999. I gave two lectures, on December 1st and 2nd, under the overall title *Jewish Philosophy as a Way of Life*. Those lectures were earlier versions of chapter 1 and chapter 4 of the present volume. Those versions were included in volumes published by Harvard University Press and Cambridge University Press, and I am grateful to those presses for permission to incorporate them (or, in the case of chapter 1, a number of paragraphs) in the present volume. Chapter 1, which was originally an essay on Rosenzweig's *Understanding the Sick and the Healthy* [*Das Büchlein vom Gutem und Kranken Menschenverstand*], has become an essay on Wittgenstein and Rosenzweig. Chapter 2 is a new essay on Rosenzweig's great book *The Star of Redemption,* and chapter 3 is an essay on Martin Buber's best-known book, *I and Thou*. The whole enterprise grew out of a course on Jewish Philosophy that I taught at Harvard University in 1997 and repeated in 1999; the impact of teaching that course on my thinking is described in the introduction. Like the course from which it grew, this is not a book for "specialists," but an attempt to make clear to a general reader what these great Jewish thinkers were saying and why I find them so impressive.

I have profited from discussions with many people. As a glance at the footnotes will show, I am especially indebted to two fine scholars who I was also lucky enough to have as graduate students and from whose work I have continued to learn: Paul Franks and Abraham Stone.

Jewish
Philosophy as
a Guide to Life

Introduction

(Autobiographical)

Religions are communal and have long histories, but religion is also a personal matter or it is nothing. So I will explain how I came to write this book in personal terms.

In my days as a graduate student at U.C.L.A., the teacher who most influenced me was Hans Reichenbach, and my interests, like his, were centered on scientific method, scientific epistemology, and philosophy of physics. After I received my Ph.D., my interests broadened somewhat, but my first few publications (outside of pure mathematical logic, a field in which I was also active), were devoted mainly to philosophy of science.[1] So how do I come, fifty-five years later, to be writing about three religious philosophers (arguably, the greatest Jewish philosophers of the twentieth century) Martin Buber, Franz Rosenzweig, and Emmanuel Levinas?

Joining a "Minyan"
The story goes back to 1975. By that time my philosophical interests had considerably broadened, but prior to that year

they still did not include religion or Judaism. But 1975 was
the year that the older of my two sons announced that he
wanted to have a bar mitzvah! Although I had never be-
longed to a "minyan" (a Jewish congregation), during the
period that I was active in opposing the Vietnam War, I
had once given an *Erev Shabbat* talk (a Friday evening talk)
at the Harvard Hillel Foundation about that war and my
reasons for opposing it, and I had a very powerful and fa-
vorable impression of the rabbi who invited me to give
it, and who participated in the discussion that followed.
Rabbi Ben-Zion Gold was not only the director of the Harvard Hillel Foundation in those years, but was also the
founder and spiritual adviser of one of the congregations
that met for worship on the Jewish Sabbath. My memory
is that there were three Hillel congregations in all, at that
time (today there are more): an Orthodox congregation,
a Reform congregation, and the one that Rabbi Gold had
founded some decades previously, which called itself then
and continues to call itself today simply "Worship and
Study" (it uses the prayer book of the Conservative movement). So when I had to find a place for my son to have his
bar mitzvah, I found it natural to go and talk to Rabbi Gold
about the possibility of Samuel having the ceremony in the
Worship and Study congregation. We agreed that my wife
and I would come to services with Samuel for a year, and
that he would study with a Jewish student (a philosophy
major whom I knew, as it happened) to prepare for the
ceremony. Long before the year was over, the Jewish service and Jewish prayers had become an essential part of
our lives, and Rabbi Gold continues to be our teacher and
friend to this day.

That an adult Jew starts attending services when one
of his children has a bar- or bat mitzvah is not at all un-
usual. But I am also a philosopher. What did I—what could

I—make *philosophically* of the religious activities that I had undertaken to be a part of?

"DAVENING" VERSUS TRANSCENDENTAL MEDITATION

Forgive a brief digression. Another part of the story is this: in those days many people were singing the praises of twenty minutes of something called Transcendental Meditation per day. Although I am sure that many of those people do find it very beneficial, something in me rebelled (perhaps unreasonably). I thought: well, in *twenty minutes* I can *daven* (say the traditional Jewish prayers). Why do I need to try something that comes from another religion? So I started to *daven* every morning (or afternoon, if I didn't find time in the morning), as I still do. I appreciate that what "davening" does to or in one's soul must be very different from what Transcendental Meditation does; be that as it may, I found it to be a transformative activity, and it quickly became an indispensable part of the "religious activities" that I just referred to.

THE TENSION BETWEEN PHILOSOPHY AND RELIGION IN MY LIFE

But to return to the question, what did I make *philosophically* of the religious activities that I had undertaken to be a part of? The question has no final answer, because it is one I am still struggling with, and will very likely struggle with as long as I am alive. But the following words, which appear on page 1 of my *Renewing Philosophy*,[2] represent one moment in that struggle:

> As a practicing Jew, I am someone for whom the religious dimension of life has become increasingly important, although it is not a dimension that I know how to philosophize about except by indirection, and the study of science has loomed large in my life. In fact, when I first began to teach philosophy, back

in the early 1950s, I thought of myself as a philosopher of science and a mathematical logician (although I included philosophy of language and philosophy of mind in my generous interpretation of the phrase "philosophy of science"). Those who know my writings from that period may wonder how I reconciled my religious streak, which existed to some extent even back then, and my general scientific materialist worldview at that time. The answer is that I didn't reconcile them. I was a thoroughgoing atheist, and I was a believer. I simply kept these two parts of myself separate.

Although by the time I wrote *Renewing Philosophy* my "scientific materialism" had been replaced by a more humanistic philosophical outlook (in that book, my heroes were Wittgenstein and Dewey), in *Renewing Philosophy* I did not attempt to deal directly with the question of how, as a philosopher, I was to make sense of the religious side of my life. If I "philosophized by indirection" about that question in that book, it was via the two chapters on Wittgenstein's "Lectures on Religious Belief,"[3] in which I sympathetically expounded Wittgenstein's view of religious language. As I explained, there is a difficult question that an interpreter of those lectures has to address:[4]

> If Wittgenstein is not saying one of the standard things about religious language [and I had already argued he wasn't doing that]—for example, that it expresses false pre-scientific theories, or that it is non-cognitive, or that it is emotive, or that it is incommensurable [with ordinary descriptive language]—then what is he saying, and how is it possible for him to avoid all of these standard alternatives? Still more important, how does he think we, including those of us who are not religious (and I don't think Wittgenstein himself ever succeeded in recovering the Christian faith in which he was raised, although it was always a possibility for him that he might), are to think about re-

ligious language? What sort of a model is Wittgenstein offering us for reflection on what is always a very important, very difficult, and sometimes very divisive part of human life?

According to the interpretation I went on to offer, Wittgenstein did not, in the end, offer a single "model." Rather he tried to get his students to see how, for *homo religiosus,* the meaning of his or her words is not exhausted by criteria in a public language, but is deeply interwoven with the sort of person the particular religious individual has chosen to be and with pictures that are the foundation of that individual's life.

Wittgenstein wrote that "I am not a religious man: but I cannot help seeing every problem from a religious point of view."[5] For Wittgenstein, the problem was to combat simplistic ideas of what is to be religious, both on the part of antireligious people and on the part of religious people, and (I believe) to get us to see the spiritual value that he thought was common to all religions. But he did not face my problem, which was to reflect on a religious commitment that I had made. *Renewing Philosophy* continued to defer addressing it. I had come to accept that I could have two different "parts of myself," a religious part and a purely philosophical part, but I had not truly reconciled them. Some may feel I still haven't reconciled them—in a conversation I recently had with an old friend, I described my current religious standpoint as "somewhere between John Dewey in *A Common Faith* and Martin Buber." I am still a religious person, and I am still a naturalistic philosopher (which, by the way, the three philosophers I describe in this little book were not). A naturalistic philosopher, but not a reductionist. Physics indeed describes the properties of matter in motion, but reductive naturalists forget that the world has many levels of form, including the level of morally significant human action, and the idea that all of these can be reduced to the level of physics I believe to be a fantasy. And, like the classic pragmatists, I do not see reality as morally indifferent: reality, as Dewey saw, *makes demands* on us. Values may be created by human beings and human cultures, but I see them as made in response to demands that we do not create. It is reality that determines whether our responses are adequate or inadequate. Similarly, my friend Gordon Kaufman may be right in saying that "the available God" is a human construct, but I am sure he would agree that we construct our images of God in response to demands that we do not create, and that it is not up to us whether our responses are adequate or inadequate.[6]

TEACHING JEWISH PHILOSOPHY

What did help me to reconcile these sides of myself, although not in any way I anticipated, and probably not in a way that is "right" for most others, was my decision in 1997 to offer a course in Jewish philosophy. That course included the three Jewish philosophers (or 3¼, if we count Wittgenstein as ¼!) with which this book deals. While they certainly have disagreements, what I found they had in common was related to what I had seen in Wittgenstein's "Lectures on Religious Belief": namely, the idea that for a religious person *theorizing* about God is, as it were, beside the point. Buber expresses this profoundly (though certainly not simply!) when he writes (*I and Thou*, p. 159):

> Man receives, and what he receives is not a "content" but a presence, a presence as strength. This presence and this strength include three elements that are not separate but may nevertheless be contemplated as three. First, the whole abundance of actual reciprocity, of being admitted, of being associated while one is altogether unable to indicate what that is

like with which one is associated, nor does association make life any easier for us—it makes life heavier, but heavy with meaning. And this is second: the inexpressible confirmation of meaning. It is guaranteed. Nothing, nothing can henceforth be meaningless. The question about the meaning of life has vanished. But if it were still there, it would not require an answer. You do not know how to point to or define the meaning, you lack any formula or image for it, and yet it is more certain for you than the sensations of your senses. What could it intend with us, what does it desire from us, being revealed and surreptitious? It does not wish to be interpreted by us—for that we lack the ability—only to be done by us. This comes third: it is not the meaning of "another life" but that of this life, not of a "beyond" but of this our world, and it wants to be demonstrated by us in this life and this world. The meaning can be received but not experienced; it cannot be experienced, but it can be done; and this is what it intends with us. The guarantee does not wish to remain shut up within me, it wants to be born into the world by me. But even as the meaning itself cannot be transferred or expressed as a universally valid and generally acceptable piece of knowledge, putting it to the proof in action cannot be handed on as a valid ought; it is not prescribed, not inscribed on a tablet that could be put up over everybody's head. The meaning we receive can be put to the proof in action only by each person in the uniqueness of his being and the uniqueness of his life.

I repeat: our "three Jewish philosophers" certainly do not agree completely, nor can any of them be summarized in a few words. This introduction is simply a way of indicating how one person who is religious but averse to "ontotheology" has found them helpful. But I believe that all of us who feel attached to religion (and, perhaps, to the Jewish tradition in particular), but are unwilling to see that attachment as requiring us to turn our backs on modernity can find spiritual inspiration in the different ways

in which these three writers, who were simultaneously exemplary human beings and exemplary thinkers, resolved
the conflicts that go with our predicament.

A last word: a friend recently asked me whether this
book would be "for a general audience." The answer is that
this book is an attempt to help the general reader, especially the general reader who will go on and read one or
more of these thinkers, to understand the strange concepts
and terms that appear in their works, and to avoid common mistakes in reading them. In that sense, it is emphati-
cally "for a general reader." But the books of a Buber, a
Rosenzweig, and a Levinas *are* difficult, and an explanation of the difficulties has to deal with difficult matters. So
a more qualified reply would be: it is for a general reader
who is motivated and willing to struggle with difficult—
spiritually difficult—ideas.

1 | Rosenzweig and Wittgenstein

In 1997 a long-lost notebook of Wittgenstein's was published under the title *Denkbewegungen* (Thought-movements).[1] Wittgenstein had recorded this notebook in Cambridge in the years 1930–1932 and then again at Skjolden in Norway in 1936–1937.

The first remark in the notebook (in my translation) reads: "Without some courage, one cannot write a sensible remark about oneself." The second remark consists of just three words: "I believe sometimes" [*Ich glaube manchmal*] (19).

Ludwig Wittgenstein is not a "Jewish philosopher," despite his Jewish ancestry.[2] He came, after all, from a family that had been Christian for two generations, and whose own religious reflections, although certainly relevant to those who think about the philosophy of religion, were rarely[3] on the Jewish religion, about which there is no reason to suppose he had any substantial knowledge.

Nonetheless, I am going to discuss a certain similarity I find in Wittgenstein's attitudes toward philosophy and those of Franz Rosenzweig, one of the best-known Jewish philosophers of the twentieth century.[4]

Wittgenstein is often thought of as virtually a "debunker" of philosophy, an "antiphilosopher," whose mission was to expose as confusions the problems that are of major concern to professional philosophers. And in fact, in *Philosophical Investigations*, §464 he himself described the aim of his later philosophy in this way: "to take you from something which is disguised nonsense to something which is undisguised nonsense," and thus to show that the "disguised nonsense"—the grand philosophical "positions"—that so enchanted us was really patent nonsense all along. It is for this reason that Peter Gordon has criticized me for daring to compare Wittgenstein to Rosenzweig (in a book I very much admire, nonetheless). For Gordon, Wittgenstein is simply a philosopher who "meant to argue . . . that philosophy is a disease, and that we require only a therapy that will remind us of those common meanings that generally worked for us when we were going on about our daily and unphilosophical affairs."[5] Needless to say, I would never have made the comparison I did, and that I shall repeat in the present volume, if I thought this was an accurate description of Wittgenstein.

In fact, this is an erroneous way to view Wittgenstein, as it considers his main concern to be that which is discussed in departments of philosophy.[6] But the tendency to become enchanted with nonsense, and to try to force reality—or, as Rosenzweig will say, Man, World, and God—to allow itself to be seen through the lens of inappropriate pictures, is neither the monopoly nor the creation of professional philosophy. What concerned Wittgenstein was something that he saw as lying deep in our lives with language (and he certainly did not think one could be "cured" of it once and for all, and certainly not by simply being reminded "of those common meanings that generally worked for us when we were going on about our daily and unphilosophical affairs").[7] If one really understands Wittgenstein, then one will see that the need for and the value of escaping the grip of inappropriate conceptual pictures is literally ubiquitous. The pursuit of clarity that Wittgenstein's work was meant to exemplify needs to go on *whenever* we engage in serious reflection. If this idea is grasped, we will see that far from being a way of bringing an end to philosophy, it represents a way to bring philosophical reflection to areas in which we often fail to see anything philosophical at all.

Moreover—and this, I believe, is of utmost importance for understanding Wittgenstein—Wittgenstein never accepted the facile idea that *religion* is essentially a conceptual confusion or collection of confusions. To be sure, there are confusions to which religious people are subject, ranging from superstition to a temptation on which Wittgenstein remarks more than once in his *Nachlass,* the temptation to make religion into a *theory* rather than (what he thought it should be) a deep-going way of life. This is a temptation that Kierkegaard devoted much of his writing to combating as well, and is, I believe, one reason for Wittgenstein's lifelong interest in Kierkegaard. But to consider religion as *essentially* "prescientific thinking," as something that must be simply rejected as nonsense after "the Enlightenment," is itself an example of a conceptual confusion for Wittgenstein, an example of being in the grip of a picture. This is why Wittgenstein attacked the way in which anthropologists were viewing primitive religion decades before it became "politically correct" to do so,[8] and the notes that we have of his fascinating "lectures on religious belief"[9] show that he was largely concerned to *defamiliarize* religious belief, to get us to see how unique a way of living and a way of conceptualizing it is. It is not that Wittgenstein was against enlightenment (without the capital *E*); it would be more accurate to say that he attacked the antireligious aspect of the "Enlightenment with a capital *E*" in the name of enlightenment itself.[10]

I began with a quotation from Wittgenstein. My next quoted comment is from the first-century Jewish philosopher, Philo of Alexandria. I encountered his remark in a favorite book—Pierre Hadot's *Philosophy as a Way of Life.*[11] In this brilliant collection of essays, one of the great historians of ancient philosophy argues that we fundamentally misunderstand the nature of *all* ancient philosophical schools if we think of ancient *philosophia* as the academic philosophy of modern or even late-medieval times. He uses the following words of Philo's to illustrate the idea of philosophy as "a mode of existing-in-the-world, which had to be practiced at each instant; and the goal of which was to transform the whole of the individual's life":[12]

> Every person—whether Greek or barbarian—who is *in training for wisdom,* leading a blameless irreproachable life, chooses neither to commit injustice nor return it to others, but to avoid the company of busybodies, and hold in contempt the places where they spend their time—courts, councils, marketplaces, assemblies—in short, every kind of meeting or reunion of thoughtless people. . . . Such people consider the whole world as their city, and its citizens are the companions of wisdom; they have received their civic rights from virtue, which has been entrusted with presiding over the universal commonwealth. To be sure, there are only a small number of such people; they are like embers of wisdom kept smoldering in our

cities so that virtue may not altogether be snuffed out and disappear from our race. But if only people everywhere felt the same way as this small number, and became as nature meant for them to be: blameless, irreproachable, and *lovers of wisdom*, rejoicing in the beautiful just because it is beautiful, and considering that there is no other good besides it . . . then our cities would be brimful of happiness.

Pierre Hadot is no philosophical reactionary. He does not believe that we can simply return to one or another of the ancient philosophical schools. But he does believe that the ancient idea of transforming one's way of life and one's understanding of one's place in the larger scheme of things and in the human community is one that we must not lose. Philosophy certainly needs analysis of arguments and logical techniques, but is in danger of forgetting that these were originally in the service of this very idea.

I have begun with this idea, the idea of philosophy (or *philosophia*) as a way of life and not an academic discipline, because three philosophers I shall be discussing in this small book—Franz Rosenzweig, Martin Buber, and Emmanuel Levinas—are thinkers who very much represent the ancient tradition that Hadot writes about. I also believe, even if it is less obvious on the surface, that Ludwig Wittgenstein is of the same vein.

I already mentioned that for Wittgenstein religion, at its best, was not a *theory*. He was aware, of course, that religion often includes belief in miracles, or in an afterlife, or both. But even these beliefs, he argued, were not like scientific beliefs; for Wittgenstein "words only have meaning in the stream of life,"[13] and the role that such beliefs play in the life of the believer is wholly different from the role that empirical beliefs play.[14] The idea that religion can either be criticized or defended by appeals to scientific fact seemed to him a mistake. And I am sure that Wittgenstein, like Kierkegaard, would have regarded the idea of "prov-ing" the truth of the Jewish or the Christian or the Muslim religion by "historical evidence" as a profound confusion of realms, a confusion of the inner transformation in one's life that he saw as the true function of religion, with the goals and activities of scientific explanation and prediction. And I believe one finds a very similar attitude expressed when Rosenzweig discusses revelation. For example, in his great open letter to Martin Buber titled "The Builders," Rosen-zweig attributes to Samson Raphael Hirsch (1808–1888), the great founder of neo-orthodoxy in Germany, the claim that the giving of the Torah at Sinai is a historical fact.[15] Rosenzweig's response is interesting. He does not deny that traditional Jews believed in this "fact," but he questions whether traditional Jews were concerned with the episte-mological question "why believe in Judaism," and whether they had just *one* reason for their way of life:

But for those living without questions," he writes, "this reason for keeping the Law was only one among others, and probably not the most cogent. No doubt the Torah, both written and oral, was given Moses on Sinai, but was it not created before the creation of the world? [Rosenzweig here and in the rest of this passage is referring to stories contained in the Talmud and midrash]. Written against a background of shining fire in let-ters of somber flame? And was not the world created for its sake? And did Adam's son Seth not found the first house of study for the teaching of the Torah? And did not the patriarchs keep the Law for half a millennium before Sinai? . . .

The "only" of orthodoxy should no more frighten us away from the Law than the "only" of liberalism . . . Judaism in-cludes these "onlies," but not in the sense of "onlies." The prob-lem of the Law cannot be dispatched by *merely affirming or denying* the pseudo-historical theory of its origin or the pseudo-juristic theory of its power to obligate, theories which Hirsch's orthodoxy made the foundation of a rigid and narrow structure, unbeautiful despite its magnificence. Similarly as with [Jewish] teaching, which cannot be dispatched by affirming or denying the pseudo-logical theory of the unity of God, or the pseudo-ethical theory of the love of one's neighbor, with which Geiger's[16] liberalism painted the façade of the new business or apartment house of emancipated Jewry. These are pseudo-historical, pseudo-juristic, pseudo-logical, pseudo-ethical motives: for a miracle does not constitute history, a people is not a juridical fact, martyrdom is not an arithmetical problem, and love is not social. We can reach both the teachings and the Law only by realizing that we are still on the very first lap of the way, *and by taking every step upon it ourselves.*[17]

In a similar vein, Rosenzweig wrote, "It would be necessary [for the person who has succeeded in saying "nothing Jewish is alien to me"] to free himself from those stupid claims that would impose 'Juda-ism' on him as a canon of definite, circumscribed 'Jewish duties' (vulgar orthodoxy), or 'Jewish tasks' (vulgar Zionism), or 'God forbid' 'Jewish ideas' (vulgar liberalism)."[18] But in "The Builders" and in other writings as well, Rosenzweig expresses disagreements with Buber's too antinomian version of Judaism as well as with Hirsch's too rigid one and Abraham Geiger's too intellectual one. Thus in his most famous work, *The Star of Redemption,*[19] Rosenzweig writes, "The presentness of the miracle of revelation is and remains its *content;* its historicity, however, is its ground and warrant."[20] The first part of this sentence formulates a point of agreement with the dialogic philosophy of Rosenzweig's good friend, Martin Buber; the second part insists that subjective experiences of presentness must show their meaning and warrant in history, which is something Buber never says.[21] Judaism must not be reduced to a dead set of observances, or even to a modern set of slogans or an ideology; on the other hand, Judaism is nothing with-

out historic continuity. Whereas Buber constantly dichoto-
mizes, separating Judaism, and, in fact, every religion, into
meaningful elements, which he identifies with, first, an
a-conceptual and, indeed, unconceptualizable moment of
dialogic relationship to God, the famous I/Thou moment,
and, secondly (as we shall see in chapter 3), the trans-
formatory effects of that moment upon one's subsequent
life in the "It-world," and meaningless elements, which he
identifies with dogmas and rules, Rosenzweig stresses in-
terdependence. *Gesetz* (Law), Rosenzweig tells Buber in
"The Builders," may not have religious meaning, but it always has the potential to become something more than
Gesetz, to become *Gebot* (divine bidding). After all, Jewish
education, which Buber values as much as Rosenzweig, is
not a matter of "I/Thou" experiences. But we go through
the "dry" spells, the preliminaries, the study of biblical
and postbiblical Hebrew and Aramaic, the acquisition of
facts, and so on, for the sake of what they make possible:
the genuine *learning* which justifies all the hard work that
came before. Similarly, keeping a "mitzvah" (a part of the
Jewish Law) can, as a result of our "inertia," seem mere
legislation, mere *Gesetz,* but as a result of our study and de-
votion, our attentiveness and openness to the divine, it can
also become a divine command, a *Gebot.* Law, in its essential duality as *Gesetz*-potential-*Gebot* is not to be seen as a
meaningless shell that has crystallized (or ossified) around
the living heart of Judaism, which is how Buber (at the
time Rosenzweig wrote "The Builders") seemed to see it.

Rosenzweig and Metaphysics

Most of us who try to learn about Rosenzweig begin with
his magnum opus, *The Star of Redemption,* and I shall defer my discussion of that work (or rather, of a part of that
work) to the next chapter. In the present chapter, I shall

discuss a much more accessible work, the charming little book titled *Understanding the Sick and the Healthy*.[22] Rosenzweig's philosophy is sometimes characterized as "existentialist," and the "target" of *Understanding the Sick and the Healthy* has often been taken to be "German idealist philosophy." The first of these characterizations is correct, provided one's paradigm of existentialism is the religious existentialism of, say, Kierkegaard's *Concluding Unscientific Postscript*, or even the highly personal existentialism of Nietzsche before *The Genealogy of Morals* and *The Will to Power*, rather than the more tendentious and phenomenological existentialism of Sartre. It is also true that a major target of *The Star of Redemption* was Hegel's philosophy. But to think that the satirical description of metaphysics in *Understanding the Sick and the Healthy* was only directed against German Idealism is to miss something very important: that Rosenzweig's attack in this book, just as much as Wittgenstein's, is an attack on a pervasive philosophical illusion, an illusion that Rosenzweig describes as the illusion that philosophy can deliver knowledge of "essences" (a knowledge unknown to ordinary common sense). That is why in *Understanding the Sick and the Healthy*, Rosenzweig mockingly describes ideas drawn from materialism, empiricism, positivism, Hans Vaihinger's then well-known philosophy of "As If" [*Als Ob*],[23] and not just Idealist ideas. Moreover, *Understanding the Sick and the Healthy* was intended for a general reader, and Rosenzweig certainly did not think that the typical assimilated German Jew of his time was in danger of becoming a convert to Hegelian or post-Hegelian metaphysics. What "philosophy" represents in Rosenzweig's *Understanding the Sick and the Healthy* is not a technical subject at all, but a temptation to which all who think of themselves as religious may be subject at one time or another. "If this were merely some philosopher's personal concern," Rosenzweig writes, "we would not object; there are so few philosophers, even taking into account the assorted breeds. But as it happens any man can trip over himself and find himself following the trail of philosophy" (42). The temptation to "follow the trail of philosophy" that Rosenzweig speaks of here is, I believe, the temptation to substitute *words,* especially words that have no religious content because they have no internal relation to a genuine religious life, for that kind of life. This is the very temptation that Kierkegaard was centrally concerned to combat. Kierkegaard did not combat the temptation to substitute abstract talk for actually living the religious life because he imagined that most nineteenth-century Danish Christians were about to become metaphysicians, any more than Rosenzweig thought that most German Jews of his time were about to become Idealist philosophers. Like Wittgenstein and Kierkegaard, Rosenzweig viewed metaphysics as an exaggerated form of a temptation, indeed, a "disease," to which we are *all* subject.

THE ABSURDITY OF METAPHYSICS[24]

The similarity between Rosenzweig's criticism of philosophy and that of the later Wittgenstein extends also to their criticism of the metaphysician's search for an account of the "essence" of things. Both regarded this as a hopeless search not because it is too *difficult* to find the essence of things, but because the project is, in some sense, *absurd.* Wittgenstein and Rosenzweig each directs us away from the chimera of a philosophical account of the "essence" of this or that to the ordinary use we make of our words. At the same time, there is an obvious difference in their projects: for Wittgenstein, returning to the ordinary use of our words is to be aided by an account of that use, by a "grammatical investigation." There is no such project in Rosenzweig; indeed, *Understanding the Sick and the Healthy,* taken by itself, can seem—*must* perhaps seem, if taken apart from what Rosenzweig has written elsewhere—as advice to turn our backs on philosophy once and for all. Yet, as Wittgenstein recognized, if there is a way past philosophy in the sense of absurd metaphysics, it must lead through philosophy in a different sense. Did Rosenzweig really not know this?

It is clear from what Rosenzweig wrote elsewhere (I shall give some examples later in this chapter) that he was fully aware of the need for another sort of philosophy. And I suspect, although I cannot of course prove, that the reason he decided not to publish the *Büchlein* may well have been precisely that, taken by itself, it seems anti-philosophical. Yet, if one sees it as a Kierkegaardian work, as a work that represents not the whole religious and existential personality of the author, but rather, as is the case with Kierkegaard's famous pseudonymous works, a work that tries to capture one particular "slant" on the religious life (a slant that is and has to be one-sided, but which is important as a corrective to the disease I described), one can understand both the quasi-fictional device it employs (narrating the course of a "disease" and its "cure" by a "sanatorium") and its deliberate one-sidedness.

The absurdity of metaphysics is, accordingly, not something that Rosenzweig *argues* for, as Wittgenstein *argues* that one or another metaphysical explanation of how it is possible to follow a rule, or possible to refer to things, collapses into absurdity when carefully probed, but rather something that he tries to make us *feel* by ironic redescription. (Although the Jewish religious sensibility is very different from the Christian, the devices of irony and parable remind one of *The Pilgrim's Progress.* Indeed, a possible alternative title for *Understanding the Sick and the Healthy* might have been *The Patient's Progress.*) Thus Rosenzweig's first example of a philosopher's search for essences is the deliberately absurd one of a philosopher seeking to know the essence of *a particular piece of butter:*

> Let us return to the example of the pound of butter. If we imagine the mental process of the buyer, we discover two possibilities: either he left home with the intention of buying, or he decided to do so when he passed the shop. Both possibilities have one thing in common—the slab of butter he finally buys is a very definite slab. Now, when did it become that particular piece? The instant the man at the counter sliced it. Or, perhaps, even earlier. If the latter, it may have happened when he discovered the butter in the shop window. What had it been previous to this? Nothing. And if the buyer did set out from home with the intention of buying butter, was it only butter in general that he had in mind? Certainly not. (47)

Rosenzweig is well aware that philosophy journals do not contain papers about "the essence of butter." Yet one can easily imagine a present-day philosophy conference at which the following arguments are advanced:

> (Prof. A:) Suppose I want a slab of butter. It could be that, unknown to me, there is no butter in existence—it was all destroyed a few minutes ago. But I still want a slab of butter. That is true whether there actually exist slabs of butter or not. So the expression "a slab of butter" cannot have its normal function of referring to slabs of (actual) butter in "I want a slab of butter." What "I want a slab of butter" actually means is that I want there to be an X such that X is in my possession and X has the *attribute* Being a Slab of Butter. The expression "slab of butter" has what Frege called an "oblique" sense and reference. It really refers to the *attribute* Being a Slab of Butter when it occurs as the object of the verb "to want."
>
>   (Prof. B:) Talk of "attributes" invokes immaterial, mysterious, hard to identify Abstract Entities. All that is mystery-

mongering. What the sentence means might be expressed by saying, "I want-true the sentence 'I have a slab of butter'."

(Prof. C:) What of third-person sentences, such as "John wants a slab of butter"?

(Prof. B:) That means: John wants-true "I have a slab of butter" spoken by John.

(Prof. C:) So "Pierre wants a slab of butter" means "Pierre wants-true the *English sentence* "I have a slab of butter" spoken by Pierre? What if Pierre doesn't know English?

[Recall Rosenzweig: "If a philosopher, however, should turn his back on our slab of butter, because the French call it *beurre*, the proper place for him would be an institution accommodating philosophers exclusively" (53)].

(Prof. D:) I suggest: "X wants a slab of butter" means "X wants true some sentence which stands in the relation of synonymy to the following English sentence. 'I have a slab of butter.'"

Of course, the participants at such a conference would probably deny that they are seeking the "essence" of butter. They would say that what they are looking for is "the right semantics for 'want-sentences'." But the notion of "the right semantics" in play here is quite obviously an *essentialist* one. The "right semantics" does not have to represent a way any actual speaker actually *understands* such a sentence; it only has to correspond to philosopher's "intuitions." Contemporary "semantics" is often just old-fashioned metaphysics in disguise.[25]

(It is instructive to compare the above Rube Goldberg accounts of the "semantics" of the verb "want," with Wittgenstein's straightforward remarks about wishes (*Philosophical Investigation* §440–441):

440. Saying "I should like an apple" does not mean: I believe an apple will quell my feeling of nonsatisfaction. *This* proposition is not an expression of a wish but of nonsatisfaction.

441. By nature and by a particular training, a particular education, we are disposed to give spontaneous expression to wishes in certain circumstances. . . . In this game the question whether I know what I wish before my wish is fulfilled cannot arise at all. And the fact that some event stops my wishing does not mean that it fulfills it. Perhaps I should not have been satisfied if my wish had been satisfied.

What makes the butter I buy "the butter I wanted," if it is, is that I *describe* the butter I buy as "what I wanted." There is nothing in the butter itself, nor in the feelings of satisfaction/nonsatisfaction and so on, that accompany the purchasing and eating of the butter which makes the butter "the object of the desire" apart from what Wittgenstein calls the language game and Rosenzweig calls "the name." And "the name" functions perfectly well without the help of any essence. As Rosenzweig puts it:

I transform the representation of my wish, as yet resembling the image in my memory, into what I see in the shop window. If we consider the matter without prejudice, we observe that after this change has taken place, nothing but the word "butter" remains the same. Is this all, then, nothing but a mere word, a name? All else has changed; the name remains. This is the first fact that must be stated. And what do we gain by such a statement? Above all, we make sure that no one is tempted to assume that the name is the "essence" of the thing. (48)

But Not Nominalism

It is important, however, not to take Rosenzweig's (or, again, Wittgenstein's) rejection of the search for essences as itself a positive metaphysical claim. The danger is, perhaps, more easily seen if we change our example of a metaphysical problem to, say, the famous "problem of personal identity." Indeed, Rosenzweig does clearly have this

problem in mind when he writes, concerning "the court-
ship which precedes marriage,"

> Since time must elapse, the answer is unavoidably given by an-
> other person than the one who was asked, and it is given to
> one who has changed since he asked it . . . a whole lifetime is
> involved in question and answer. The lovers dare not deny, not
> even Romeo and Juliet, that changes, involving both of them,
> will inevitably take place. Nevertheless they do not hesitate.
> Indeed, the man who proposes and the woman who replies
> do not reflect upon these vicissitudes. They cling to the un-
> changeable. What is the unchangeable? Unbiased reflection
> reveals once more that it is only a name. (49)

If we make the mistake of supposing that Rosenzweig is
here making a metaphysical claim—say, the metaphysical
claim that there is nothing that the different things gathered
under a name really have in common ("Nominalism")—
this could be taken to say that what we refer to as a "person," as "John," say, or "Sally," is really a succession of
different persons; indeed, the contemporary philosopher
Derek Parfit has argued for just this point of view. According to Parfit,[26] each of my momentary selves, my "time-
slices," has the right to be considered a different individual, and the idea that the self that will be called "Hilary
Putnam" in a week's time is in any sense more "identical"
to me than is a perfect stranger thousands of miles away
is just a persistent illusion. But this view is just as metaphysical as the view it opposes, the view that there is some
self-identical entity, some "substance," in traditional metaphysical terminology, that is present as long as I am myself, and which is my "essence." In traditional religious
thought, and also in the psychology of Descartes and other
Rationalist philosophers, this substance was identified with

an immaterial soul; but even if there are/were immaterial souls, could *they* not consist of different (immaterial) substances at different times? And would it make any difference to our personal identities if they did? And if there are no immaterial souls, does it make any difference to our personal identities if our bodies consist of different matter at different times?

Both Locke and Kant answered "no"; but they did not deny, as Parfit does, that it makes sense to think of myself as the same person at different times. Nor does Rosenzweig. Indeed, as Rosenzweig points out, thinking this way is essential to our lives. As he writes, "common sense in action is concerned that the name, not the 'essence', remain."[27] Or as Wittgenstein might have put it, "In this game the question whether the person we call 'Sally' is 'numerically identical' to her former self cannot arise at all."

I mentioned Locke and Kant, and if I may be permitted to digress, it is interesting to see how they each made a similar point. For Locke, what makes me the very person who lived in such and such a town as a small boy, who went to such and such a high school and college and had such and such friends, who got married, worked at various places, wrote and said various things, and so on, who did such-and-such and is now ashamed of it or proud of it, and so on, is that I acknowledge those events as happening to me and my memories of them as my own. This is another way of making the point that "common sense in action" has no choice but to rely on the language game. For Kant, rational thought itself depends on the fact that I regard my thoughts, experiences, memories, and the like as all *mine* (the fact that I prefix the "I think" to all of them, not just at the time but also retrospectively.) To illustrate Kant's point, imagine yourself going through a very simple form of reasoning, say "Boiling water hurts if

you stick your finger in it; this is boiling water; so it will
hurt if I stick my finger in this." If the "time-slice" of me
that thought "Boiling water hurts if you stick your finger
in it" was one person, person A, and the "time-slice" that
thought the minor premise, "This is boiling water" is a different person, person B, and the person that thought the
"conclusion," "It will hurt if I stick my finger in this" was
yet a third person, person C, then that conclusion was not
warranted; indeed, the sequence of thoughts was not an
argument at all, since the thoughts were thoughts of different thinkers, none of whom had any reason to be bound
by what the others thought or had thought.[28] We are *responsible* for what we have thought and done in the past,
responsible *now*, intellectually and practically, and that is
what makes us *thinkers*, rational agents in a world, at all.
Kant, like Locke, can be seen as making the point that the
"game" of thinking of my thoughts and actions at different
times as *mine* does not depend on a metaphysical premise about "self-identical substances," and is nonetheless a
game that we cannot opt out of as long as we are engaged
in "common sense in action." Whereas Nominalism leaves
us without any coherent conception of ourselves and our
lives at all, *rejecting the question* that both the Rationalist
Psychologist and the Nominalist try to answer directs our
attention back to the conceptions that really inform those
lives. These thinkers insist that the question: "How many
self-identical substances do I consist of" is a question that
diverts our attention away from the real issue, the issue of
what is required for "common sense in action" [*der gesunde
Menschenverstand in seinem Handeln*].

GOD

Rosenzweig is, however, a *religious* thinker. The question
he is concerned with—concerned with *vitally*, as a living

practical question—is: what does "common sense in action" mean for a religious human being? By treating Man, the World, and God as three "mountains" that his "patient" glimpses from his sanatorium, Rosenzweig means to suggest that a proper relation to God no more depends on a *theory*, on an intellectual conception of what God "really is," or a grasp of the "essence" of God, than does a proper relation to other human beings or to the world depend on a theory of man or the world. Again, a comparison with Wittgenstein may help in grasping the thought. In his masterful exposition and development of Wittgenstein's thought, *The Claim of Reason*, Stanley Cavell interprets Wittgenstein as finding a "truth in skepticism," albeit one whose significance the skeptic distorts and misunderstands. It is true that we do not "know" that there is a world and that there are other people, on Cavell's interpretation, but not because (this is the skeptic's misunderstanding) we "don't know" these things. In ordinary circumstances, circumstances in which neither doubt nor justification is called for, our relation to the familiar things in our environment, the pen in our hand or the person in pain whom we are consoling, is not one of either "knowing" or "not knowing." Rather, Cavell suggests it is one of *acknowledging* their reality (or, sadly, failing to acknowledge it). Our task is not to acquire a "proof" that "there is an external world" or that our friend is in pain, but to *acknowledge* the world and our friend. I suggest that we read Rosenzweig, the religious thinker, as adding that it is our task to acknowledge God (indeed, as a profoundly religious thinker, albeit also a profoundly humanist thinker, Rosenzweig does not think one can acknowledge any one of the three—God, Man, and World—as they demand to be acknowledged unless one acknowledges the other two).

But like Cavell's Wittgenstein, Rosenzweig insists that acknowledging is not a matter of knowledge.

Although he has a religious sensibility,[29] Wittgenstein never calls himself a *theist*.[30] But it is clear that for him too a religion, if it is to have any value, cannot be a *theory:*

> It strikes me that a religious belief could only be something like a passionate commitment to a system of reference. Hence, although it's *belief,* it's really a way of living, or a way of assessing life. It's passionately seizing hold of *this* interpretation. Instruction in a religious faith, therefore, would have to take the form of a portrayal, a description, of that system of reference, while at the same time being an appeal to conscience [*ein in's-Gewissen-reden*]. And this combination would have to result in the pupil himself, of his own accord, passionately taking hold of the system of reference. It would be as though someone were first to let me see the hopelessness of my situation and then show me the means of rescue until, of my own accord, or not at any rate led to it by my *instructor,* I ran to it and grasped it.[31]

Fear of Life and Fear of Death

It is important that Rosenzweig's passionate attack on the quest for essences—whether the quest be for an essence of Man, an essence of the World, or for a grasp of the very essence of God—is not an attack on *wonder.* As Rosenzweig writes, "Were it a question of this gift alone, this capacity to wonder, philosophy's rightful claim to superiority could not be disputed." (*Understanding the Sick and the Healthy,* 39)

But wonder, Rosenzweig points out, however extensively (and peculiarly) it may be cultivated by philosophy, is not originally a particularly philosophical activity. Thus, almost immediately after the passage I just quoted, Rosenzweig continues, "But be that as it may, how does our philosopher know of wonder? In any case, where does he obtain the word? Does not the non-philosophizing half of mankind also wonder? The wonder of a child? The wonder of a savage? Does not wonder overcome them a hundred times—even oftener than the philosopher?" (39–40).

In that extraordinary thing called "ordinary" life, wonder arises and dissolves in the flow of life itself. Even as lovers wonder at each other, "the solution and dissolution of their wonder is at hand—the love which has befallen them. They are no longer a wonder to each other; they are in the very heart of wonder." And life "becomes numb in the face of death—and dies. The wonder is unraveled. And it was life itself that brought the solution" (both quotations are from p. 40).

As Rosenzweig sees it, the philosopher is a being who is incapable of accepting the process of life and what he calls "the passing of the numbness wonder has brought." Such a relief comes too slowly. The philosopher "does not permit his wonder, stored as it is, to be released into the flow of life. Of necessity, he must hook the 'problem' from where he stands. He has forcibly extracted thought's 'object' and 'subject' from the flow of life and he entrenches himself within them. Wonder *stagnates* [my emphasis—HP], is perpetuated in the motionless mirror of his meditation; that is in the subject. He has it well-hooked; it is securely fastened, and it persists in his benumbed immobility. The stream of life has been replaced by something submissive—statuesque, subjugated" (40–41).

A number of critics of the traditional metaphysical enterprise have noted that the philosopher seeks an imaginary position, one outside the flow of time. He seeks to view everything, even himself, as if he were an "outsider," and seeks to view the world as if he were not *in* it, but to view it "from sideways on," as John McDowell has put it.[32]

By describing this imaginary position as a place outside the current, outside demands of life and the flow of time, Rosenzweig suggests that this sort of philosophy stems from a "fear to live" (102). But at the close of *Understanding the Sick and the Healthy,* just before the epilogues, Rosenzweig gives a deeper diagnosis:

> We have wrestled with the fear to live, with the desire to step outside the current; now we may discover that reason's illness was merely an attempt to elude death. Man, chilled in the full current of life, sees, like that famous Indian prince, death waiting for him. So he steps outside of life. If living means dying, he prefers not to live. (102)

It is, of course, easy for a healthy young man to call for the courage to face life, and even to face death. But, as is well known, Rosenzweig displayed his ability to live up to the demands of his own existential philosophy in a most remarkable way. *Understanding the Sick and the Healthy* was finished in July 1921. Early in 1922 the first signs of Lou Gehrig's disease appeared, and by the end of the year he was already experiencing difficulty in speaking and writing. Within a few years, he was reduced to a condition resembling that of the physicist Stephen Hawking— virtually paralyzed, and reduced to communicating by means of eye-blinks (his wife would recite the alphabet, and he would spell out words by blinking at the letter he wanted). Yet, under *these* conditions, he remained the intellectual leader of the school for adult Jewish education that he founded, translated the Bible from Hebrew into German together with Martin Buber, and produced a flood of fascinating letters and papers—letters, one must say, that remain full of confidence and free of self-pity right to the end! One's appreciation of Rosenzweig's life-attitude can only be deepened by observing how he managed to realize that attitude, and to live life to the fullest, under such a terrible handicap.

The New Thinking is "Speaking Thinking"

I claimed earlier that it is clear from what Rosenzweig wrote elsewhere that he was not simply "anti-philosophical." Rather, he is concerned with calling for a different sort of philosophy, an existential philosophy that he calls simply "the new thinking." (In an essay with that title, "The New Thinking," that he wrote in 1925 to explain the purpose and structure of *The Star of Redemption*, he lists, in addition to himself, a number of contemporaries as exponents of the "new thinking," including Martin Buber, Ferdinand Eber, Hans Ehrenberg, and Victor von Weizsäcker.)[33] But the new thinking is not the subject of *Understanding the Sick and the Healthy*—not *explicitly*, that is. What this little book artfully depicts is a certain religious attitude; one characterized by a profound but undogmatic acknowledgement of man, world, and God. It would be contrary to Rosenzweig's whole spirit to explain what that means by offering a blueprint. But before saying a word about Rosenzweig's Judaism, I wish to say a word or two about the kind of philosophy that Rosenzweig recommends in place of the kind of philosophy he so brilliantly satirizes. In this section, then, my quotations will come not from *Understanding the Sick and the Healthy*, but from a wonderful selection of Rosenzweig's letters and writings that Nahum Glatzer assembled to "present" Franz Rosenzweig's life and thought.[34]

It is clear from those letters and writings that the "new thinking" is continuous with the trajectory of Rosenzweig's life. I am not only alluding to the courage and the sense of adventure that Rosenzweig displayed under terrible adversity. Even before the onset of his paralyzing illness, in a letter to Friedrich Meinecke dated August 30, 1920, in which he rejects the offer of a university lecture-ship,[35] Rosenzweig exemplifies the attitudes he argued for in *The Star of Redemption* as well as in *Understanding the Sick and the Healthy:*

> The one thing I wish to make clear is that scholarship no longer holds the center of my attention, and that my life has fallen under the rule of a "dark drive" which I'm aware that I merely *name* by calling it "my Judaism." . . . The man who wrote *The Star of Redemption* . . . is of a very different caliber from the au-thor of *Hegel and the State*.[36] Yet when all is said and done, the new book is only—a book. I don't attach any undue impor-tance to it. The small—at times exceedingly small thing called "demand of the day"[37] which is made upon me in my position at Frankfurt, I mean . . . the struggles with people and condi-tions, have now become the core of my existence. . . . Now I only inquire when I find myself *inquired of*. Inquired of, that is, by *men* rather than by scholars. . . . [T]he questions asked by human beings have become increasingly important to me.

This distinction between the questions of scholars and the questions of human beings was central to Rosenzweig's "new thinking." In lieu of attempting an overview of the approach that Rosenzweig had in mind by that term, I shall list a few highlights:

(1) *The new thinking is "speaking thinking."* As Rosen-zweig explains this idea, "the difference between the old and the new, the 'logical' and the 'grammatical' thinking,[38] does not lie in the fact that one is silent while the other is audible, but the fact that the latter needs another person and takes time seriously—actually, these two things are identical. In the old philosophy, 'thinking' means think-ing for no one else and speaking to no one else (and here, if you prefer, you may substitute 'everyone' or the well-

known 'all the world' for 'no one'.) But 'speaking' means speaking to some one and thinking for some one. And this some one is always a quite definite some one, and he has not merely ears, like 'all the world,' but also a mouth."[39]

What Rosenzweig means by this is that in the active engagement with the *lived* philosophical or theological problems of another human being that he calls "speaking thinking," a speaker does not know in advance what he will say—or if, indeed, he will say anything. "Speech is bound by time and nourished by time and it neither can nor wants to abandon this element. It does not know in advance just where it will end. It takes its cues from others. In fact, it lives by virtue of another's life, whether that other is the one who listens to a story, answers in the course of a dialogue, or joins in a chorus."[40] In the same place, Rosenzweig daringly criticizes Plato's dialogues because in them "the thinker knows his thoughts in advance," and moreover the other is only raising the objections the author thought of himself. "This is why the great majority of philosophical dialogues—including most of Plato's—are so tedious. In actual conversations something happens."

(2) *Theology must be humanized as well as philosophy.* "Theological problems must be translated into human terms, and human problems brought into the pale of theology."[41]

(3) *We need "readiness" rather than "plans."* The task that Rosenzweig undertook to make his life work, his "vocation" in the most serious sense, was nothing less than to restore a meaningful Jewish life in a Western country, Weimar Germany, in which Jews were rapidly forgetting their Jewishness. He wanted this restoration to be undogmatic, and although his was a deeply *religious* vocation, he wanted to revive *all* forms of Jewish learning, secular as well as religious. This is a task which he saw as possess-

ing "unlimited" importance, since, for a religious Jew, it is a part of the everlasting task of preserving a "bridge" between man and God (and the image of a "bridge" is one of Rosenzweig's favorite metaphors for revelation, which he construes as an ongoing process, something that happens in each religiously lived life). At the same time, it is a task for a particular historical moment. Remarking on both of these aspects, Rosenzweig writes:

> What is intended to be of limited scope can be carried out according to a limited, clearly outlined plan—it can be "organized." The unlimited cannot be attained by organization. That which is distant can be attained only through that which is nearest at the moment. Any "plan" is wrong to begin with— simply because it is a plan. The highest things cannot be planned; for them readiness is everything. Readiness is the one thing we can offer to the Jewish individual within us, the individual we aim at.[42]

And he adds,

> Only the first gentle push of the will—and "will" is almost too strong a word—that first quite gentle push we give ourselves when in the confusion of the world we quietly say, "we Jews," and by that expression commit ourselves to the eternal pledge that, according to an old saying, makes every Jew responsible for every other Jew. Nothing more is assumed than the simple resolve to say once: "Nothing Jewish is alien to me"—and this is in itself hardly a resolve, scarcely anything more than a small impulse to look around oneself and into oneself. What each will then see no one can venture to predict.

THE HOLY AND THE PROFANE

In *Understanding the Sick and the Healthy,* the idea that the holy is not simply in opposition to the profane is expressed as a denial that the Jewish holiday is to be thought of as in opposition to the work day. We see this in the chapter titled "Convalescence" (chapter 9), when he writes (on p. 96): "It is through the holiday that the work day receives its definition. We must bear in mind that we are not dealing with something entirely distinct from the weekday world as though the serious side of life were now replaced by the elation of art."

For Rosenzweig, the importance of the Jewish holidays, the feasts and the fasts, lies precisely in their ability to relate the one who observes them to life as a whole. "Insofar as the holiday is exceptional, it merely confirms the work day. There is no superior content to the holiday. The holiday does not seek that which is absent from the work day, does not know what the work day is not capable of recognizing. It does, however, state explicitly and as a whole those things which the latter expresses only partially and occasionally. God, man, and the world are the content of the holiday, and in a perfectly everyday manner" (96).

The very next sentences express Rosenzweig's attitude with great beauty:

> The holiday knows as little as the sane, healthy work day, what God, man and the world "are." The holiday does not permit their "essences" to be disputed. It knows no remote God, no isolated man, no fenced-in world. God, man, and the world are for it in constant motion; they are in transition, the three of them constantly joining and interweaving and separating. The undulations of beseeching and receiving, receiving and thanking, go on incessantly. Man asks, God gives, the world receives and thanks—and then man asks anew. There can be no dead season, no merely localized pulsation here; the process must be continual. The holiday cannot pretend to isolate any of the three elements. It must do without the spectacle of drama, because unfortunately drama remains mere spectacle.

In *The Star of Redemption*, however, there is another aspect, one which disappears in *Understanding the Sick and the Healthy*, and, indeed, in almost all of Rosenzweig's later writing.[43] This aspect is far more Hegelian than Rosenzweig acknowledges; in fact, it seems to me to be the remnant of his former Hegelianism. It is the idea that two and only two religions—Judaism and Christianity—have genuine significance. Indeed, one may say that he grants these two religions *metaphysical* significance.

The most unfortunate aspects of *The Star of Redemption* are, in fact, its polemical remarks about religions other than these two—its scorn for Islam, for Hinduism, and so on. What Rosenzweig does in the *Star* is retain the Hegelian idea of a "world historic" religion, and argue that, indeed, Christianity is *the* world historic religion par excellence, the one fated to bring "pagan" mankind to theism, and invent a new and contrasting metaphysical dignity for Judaism—the dignity of being the only "ahistoric" religion—not ahistoric in the sense of never changing, but ahistoric in the sense that, in some metaphysical way, the changes are not "real" changes. In effect, it is as if there were an *essence* of Judaism that did not change, much as Rosenzweig would object to that way of putting it. In effect, the "world-historic" religion, Christianity, is a witness to the truth of the "ahistoric" Judaism.

Given that in his best moments Rosenzweig beautifully attacks both essentialism and historicism, I find this aspect of the *Star* depressing, and the fact that it is wholly absent in *Understanding the Sick and the Healthy* (and virtually absent from his later writing) something to be thankful for.

Above all, Rosenzweig sought to nourish an undogmatic, pluralistic, Jewish revival. He sought to teach that we are always in the presence of God, that there is essentially just one commandment, the commandment to love God,[44] and only one thing to ask for in prayer: the strength to meet "the small—at times exceedingly small thing called demand of the day" with courage and confidence.

2 | Rosenzweig on Revelation and Romance

In "The New Thinking," the essay from which I quoted in chapter 1, Rosenzweig provides valuable information about the structure and purposes of *The Star of Redemption* (published four years earlier).[1] Rosenzweig is well aware that the *Star* is a difficult book. But he thinks the difficulties the reader faces are in part common to all significant philosophical works. As he explains in this essay:[2]

> The first pages of philosophical books are met by the reader with special reverence. He believes that they are to be the basis for all that follows. Therefore he also thinks that it would suffice to refute them, in order to have refuted the whole. Hence the enormous interest in Kant's doctrine of space and time in the form in which he developed it in the beginning of the *Critique;* hence the comical attempts to "refute" Hegel with respect to the first triple-step of his *Logic,* and Spinoza with respect to his definitions.[3] And hence the helplessness of the

"general reader" [Rosenzweig uses the English words here] before philosophical books. He thinks they must be "especially logical," by which he means the dependence of each subsequent sentence on each preceding one, such that when the famous one stone is pulled out "the whole comes tumbling down." In truth, this is nowhere less the case than in philosophical books. Here a sentence does not follow from its predecessor, but, much more likely, from its successor. It will be of little help to whomever has not understood a sentence or paragraph if, in his conscientious belief that he may leave nothing behind uncomprehended, he reads it over and over again, or even starts once more from the beginning. Philosophical books defy the *ancien regime* strategy that thinks it may not leave any unconquered fortresses in the rear; they want to be conquered in a Napoleonic manner, in a bold advance on the enemy's main force, after whose defeat the small border fortresses will fall on their own. (112–113)

Rosenzweig's account of the structure of the *Star* in "The New Thinking," however, reveals an additional reason why "the *ancien regime*" strategy, of trying to understand each sentence thoroughly, or indeed each larger section, of the *Star* on its own, on a first reading, is not going to work. It will fail because there is a sense in which the whole of Part I of the *Star* is self-undermining, but this aspect cannot be seen until one has completed its reading and gone on to Part II. As "The New Thinking" tells us, "What is said [in Part One of the *Star*] is nothing other than a *reductio ad absurdum* and, at the same time, a rescue of the old philosophy" (114–115). Rosenzweig then explains "this apparent paradox," and the explanation will not surprise a reader who has read *Understanding the Sick and the Healthy* (as Rosenzweig's contemporary readers had not).[4] The explanation is that the "old philosophy," which Part I pushes to what Rosenzweig sees as its limit, tries to account for the three "mountains" of *Understanding the Sick*

and the Healthy—world, man, and God—by considering
each in abstraction from the other two, and looking for an
essence. The search has to fail. As Rosenzweig explains in
language very close to the language of *Understanding the
Sick and the Healthy*,

> All philosophy asked about "essence." It is by this question
> that it distinguishes itself from the unphilosophical thinking
> of healthy human understanding. For the latter does not ask
> itself what a thing "really" [*eigentlich*] is. It is sufficient for it to
> know that a chair is a chair; it does not it does not ask whether
> it might really [*eigentlich*] be something entirely different. Phi-
> losophy asks exactly this when asking about essence. The
> world is by no means permitted to be the world, God is by no
> means permitted to be God, man by no means permitted to be
> man, rather all must "really" be something totally different. If
> they were nothing else but actually only what they are, then
> philosophy—[heaven] forbid and forfend!—would ultimately
> be superfluous. At least a philosophy which absolutely might
> ferret out something "entirely different." (115)

If the search for an "essence" standing behind and en-
abling us to use any one of the three concepts of man,
world, God—an essence expressible in "different" words—
was the great quest of "the old philosophy," and that whole
search was misguided, is philosophy then at an end?

> In truth, these three last and first objects of all philosophizing
> [the concepts *man, world,* and *God*] are onions that one may
> pare down as much as one wants—one will also encounter
> more onion skins and not something "entirely different." Only
> thinking necessarily falls into these errant ways by virtue of
> the altering force of the little word "is." Experience, no mat-
> ter how deeply it may penetrate, discovers only the human in
> man, only worldliness in the world, only divinity in God. And
> only in God divinity, only in the world worldliness, and only
> in man the human. *Finis Philosophiae?*[5] If it were, then so much

the worse for philosophy! But I do not believe that it turns out so badly. Rather, at this point where philosophy would certainly be at an end with its thinking, experiential philosophy can begin. In any case, that is the point of my first volume [i.e., of Part I of the *Star*]. (116–117)

Here we have the answer to our question! Philosophy is not at an end, but a new kind of philosophy, "experiential philosophy" (which Rosenzweig also calls "narrative philosophy") is called for. "The second volume's [i.e., Part II's] method will have to be . . . a method of narration. In his preface to his ingenious fragment *The Ages of the World*, Schelling prophesized a narrative philosophy. [Part II] attempts to provide it" (121). It is the "narrative philosophy" of Part II that Rosenzweig describes as the "core" of his great book.[6]

When Rosenzweig explains his call for a "narrative philosophy," he begins by once again castigating the "old philosophy's" habit of trying to say what man "is," what the world "is," and what God "is," and (of course) it does so in terms that are "entirely different" (otherwise the philosopher's statement would be trivial, the philosopher thinks):

What then does it mean to narrate? He who narrates does not want to say how it really [*eigentlich*] was, but rather how it actually came about . . . the narrator never wants to show that it was really quite different—it is precisely the criterion of a bad, concept-obsessed or sensationalist historian to go for that—; rather he want to show how this and that—which is in every mouth as a concept or a name, such as the Thirty Years War or the Reformation—actually happened.

That is to say, time becomes entirely actual to him. . . . Essence want to know nothing of time. Now in [Part II of the *Star*] sequence becomes not merely important, but is the really important [matter] which is supposed to be communicated. It is already itself the new thinking of which I spoke at the beginning. If, say, the old [thinking] addressed the question whether God is transcendent or immanent, then the new [thinking] attempts to show how and when He turns from the distant into the near God, and again from the near into the distant. (121–122)

But Rosenzweig's "how and when" are not meant in a fundamentalist sense, as we shall see. The narrative he offers in Part II of *The Star of Redemption* is no more to be taken literally than is the "narrative" in Nietzsche's *Thus Spake Zarathustra*. To explain what Rosenzweig is doing, it is necessary to take note of the very special prose that goes with his "narrative philosophy."

Rosenzweig's Prose

Like Kierkegaard's, or, for that matter Nietzsche's or Emerson's, Rosenzweig's prose (in all his writings) is meant to lead the reader into an encounter with the author, one in which the reader will be profoundly changed. In this sense, it is existential prose. It is of the nature of existential prose that it has to be read more than once. As Rosenzweig has told us in the essay I have been discussing, the sentences one reads will acquire quite different meanings by the time one has read to the end (the end of each of many readings, in the case of the ideal reader). In a sense, Rosenzweig is attempting the impossible: attempting to do in writing what can really only be achieved by face-to-face conversation of the kind he calls "speaking thinking."

Not only is Rosenzweig's prose existential prose, but it is also, of course, religious prose. Indeed, it is *revelatory writing*.[7] As Paul Franks points out:

Rosenzweig—in a brief but crucially important 1928 response to the article on anthropomorphisms in the German *Encyclo-*

pedia Judaica—argues, in effect, that *the entire discourse has been conducted on the wrong basis.* It may be correct to characterize Homeric poetry as our talk about God. But it would be entirely incorrect to characterize Hebrew scripture—the Tanakh—in these terms. For the Tanakh is fundamentally *revelation*. It is not man's word *about* God, but rather God's word *to* man: "Theological experiences . . . have just this in common: they are experiences of meetings, not experiences of an objective kind like experiences of the world, not a mixture of both, like experiences between human beings. Therefore, to remain here within the precinct of experience one does not want to assert something either about God or about man, but only about an event between the two."[8]

ROSENZWEIG'S UNDERSTANDING OF REVELATION

To understand Rosenzweig's revelatory writing, then, we have to know something about his notion of revelation as "an event between the two." When Rosenzweig writes about revelation, he obviously does not assume the model of God's literally dictating words to a human secretary. On the other hand, Julius Wellhausen's "documentary hypothesis" neither disturbs him nor greatly interests him.[9] Rather, Rosenzweig rejects the idea that scientific accounts of religion—be they psychological, sociological, or historical—are or should be important to the religious life of the practicing Jew. In a letter to the "speakers of the Lehrhaus," the leaders of the Freies Jüdisches Lehrhaus of which he was one of the founders, he wrote as follows:

> Just as a student of William James knows how to put every "religious experience" into the correct cubbyhole of the psychology of religion, and a Freudian student can analyze the experience into its elements of the old but ever new story, so a student of Wellhausen will trace every commandment back to its human folkloristic origin, and a student of Max Weber de-

rive it from the special structure of a people. We know it differently, not always and not in all things, but again and again. For we know it only when—we *do*.[10]

Rosenzweig emphasizes that it is not the *truth* of all such explanations that he contests, but their religious significance:[11] "What do we know when we do? Certainly not that all these historical and sociological explanations are false. But in the light of the doing, the right doing in which we experience the reality of the Law, the explanations are of superficial and subsidiary importance."

Rosenzweig believes that revelation happened in the past, that God broke through to humanity, but that the historicity of revelation does not mean the historicity of a particular "text." But to say this is only to characterize Rosenzweig's conception negatively, not to say positively what his conception was. But, as we just saw, Rosenzweig believes that the positive conception can only be given in "narrative form," not in the form of the traditional philosophical essay. And it is a particular "narrative" that Rosenzweig offers us in Part II of the *Star*.

As I shall explain in chapter 4, I also perceive a kind of hidden narrative in Levinas's ethical philosophy. When Levinas tells us that each of us must learn to say "here I am" to the other, his "here I am" is really modeled on Abraham's *hineni*, which is what Abraham says to God when God calls on him to sacrifice his beloved son Isaac (and also, paradoxically, what he says to Isaac when they are on the way to the *Akedah* [the "sacrifice of Isaac"]).

I believe that for Rosenzweig, the moment in which Abraham says *hineni* to God will serve as the model. The clue that this is the case can be found on page 176 of *The Star of Redemption*.[12] It is true that the name *Abraham* does not appear on that page. On the surface, pp. 175–

176 are a meditation on chapter 3 of Genesis. Rosenzweig writes,

> The human being materializes as "man" [*adam* in Hebrew], it is the woman who did it [Adam's excuse, Gen. 3:12], and specifically the woman who materializes as she was given to man. And she transfers the blame to the ultimate It: it was the serpent. The soul demands to be conjured by a more powerful spell than the mere inquiry after the Thou before it will answer the I. The indefinite Thou was merely referential,[13] and so it was answered with a mere referential: the woman, the serpent. Its place is taken by the vocative, the direct address, and man is cut off from every retreat into hypostatization. The general concept of man can take refuge behind the woman or the serpent. Instead of this the call goes out to what cannot flee, to the utterly particular, the nonconceptual,[14] to something that transcends the sphere of influence of both the definite and the indefinite articles—a sphere which embraces all things if only as objects of a particular nondistinctive providence—to the proper name, the proper name which is not yet properly *his* name, not a name ["Adam"] which the man gave himself arbitrarily, but the name which God himself created for the man, and which is properly the man's only because it is the creation of the Creator. To God's "Where art Thou?" [Gen. 3:9], the man had still kept silent as defiant and blocked Self. Now, called by his name, twice, in a supreme definiteness that could not but be heard, now he answers, all spread apart, all ready, all-soul, "'Here I am'."

But Rosenzweig is playing a trick on the reader. God does *not* call Adam twice in Genesis 3! Nor does Adam answer "Here I am"! But God calls Adam *once* in Genesis 3 and calls *Abraham* in Genesis 22:1. And *Abraham* answers *hineni*, "Here I am"! Here Rosenzweig is taking the two calls as two events in the life of *adam*, man, and taking Abraham's *hineni* as the true response of *adam*, the answer which is "all spread apart, all ready, all-soul."

Each Sabbath traditional Jews recite a shorter version of the Standing Prayer [Amidah]. Traditional Jews recite the full eighteen—now nineteen—benedictions the other six days of the week. In both versions, the first benediction contains the words, "Remembering the patriarchs loving-kindness [*zeher hasdei avot*], you will bring a redeemer to their children's children for the sake of Thy name in love. O King, Thou Helper, Savior and Shield, be Thou Blessed, Shield of Abraham."

In this opening blessing, which summarizes some of the central doctrines of traditional Judaism, we see that God is depicted as remembering the patriarch's love (or, literally, their loving-kindness, *hasdei avot*). In addition, it is said that God will bring (or, more literally, *is* bringing) a redeemer in *love*. Here, the relation of God to the patriarchs and their "children's children" is portrayed as a *love relation*.

To be sure, God remembers us for other reasons as well. God is repeatedly said to be faithful to his covenant; that is, He is not a God who breaks His word or goes back on covenants. And in the Torah we are told that even though God punishes the Jewish people, God will never forget them or wipe them out completely. But the idea that God *loves* the Jewish people and that he "remembers the patriarchs" is interesting, and, for a "rational" point of view, decidedly odd. God, who is from the very beginning portrayed as "the God of all the world," is described as having, so to speak, *fallen in love* with a particular people. Moreover, this love affair seems to begin with one particular ancestor of that people, with Abraham.

Moreover, although God is said to "remember the merit" of the patriarchs, which means, of course, in particular the merit of Abraham, he seems to have picked Abraham *before* Abraham displayed that merit (or merits).

Just as a human lover is very often unable to say why he or she fell in love with the beloved, so God seems to have fallen in love with the beloved before being sure of the beloved's qualities. (Here I am ignoring the picture of God that William James said was "the product of the philosophy shop," the God of the philosophers, and am simply focusing on God as he is portrayed in narrative language in the book of Genesis.) The very first we hear of Abraham, apart from the bare facts of his genealogy, is in Genesis 12:1—"The Lord said unto Abram [who had not yet been renamed *Abraham*], "Go forth from your native land and from your father's house to the land that I will show you." And the story continues: "I will make of you a great nation, and I will bless you. I will make your name great and you shall be a blessing. I will bless those who bless you and curse him that curses you; and all the families of the earth shall bless themselves by you" (Gen. 12:2).

Perhaps God himself wondered at times whether this love was wise—at least we are told that he "tested" Abraham, with the severe test of the Akedah (and that Abraham said *hineni*). But that test came many years later. Just as we are not told why Moses was picked, although in that case we have at least been told (or rather shown) something about Moses' character as revealed in his previous deeds, so we are not told what made God "fall in love" with Abraham. (And with Sarah, judging by the great indulgence God shows her.) It is this picture of God as a lover that dominates the narrative in the section about Revelation (Book II of Part II) in the *Star*.

If we are in the position of Abraham in Rosenzweig's philosophical theology, it is, originally at least, a passive position—albeit one of being "all ready"—the position of being confronted or overwhelmed by the love of a being who is wholly Other. The whole of the "narrative philosophy" in Book II of the *Star* tells the tale of a love affair, the love affair between God and the receptive human soul.

God tells each of us, although not all of us hear the voice, "love me." This, Rosenzweig tells us, is the *only* command we receive from God. But can love be *commanded*? It is worth our while to read Rosenzweig's answer:

> Yes of course, love cannot be commanded. No third party can command it or extort it. No third part can, but the One can. The commandment to love can only proceed from the mouth of the lover. Only the lover can and does say: love me!—and he really does so. In his mouth the commandment to love is not a strange commandment; it is none other than the voice of love itself. The voice of the lover has, in fact, no word to express itself other than the commandment. (176)

If we accept the role of the beloved, and return God's love, then there are consequences, and those consequences have to do with what Rosenzweig describes as Redemption. The soul that has become God's beloved comes to desire "matrimony" (203). But "matrimony" involves the taking on of responsibilities that carry one outside a merely "interior" relation to God. To explain this, I need to say a word about what Rosenzweig sees as the greatest danger facing the soul. This danger is adumbrated in the first part of the *Star,* in which, among other things, Rosenzweig describes man apart from his relation to God (he calls this a "metaethical" description). "Metaethical" man—and we are all said to be in danger of relapsing into the position of metaethical man—suffers from a kind of confinement in himself, and this is what Rosenzweig sees as the tragedy that threatens everyone, the tragedy of being completely enclosed in oneself. (I am reminded here of Auden's lines, "The error bred in the bone / of each woman and each man / what each one secretly craves / not universal love, but to be loved alone"; and also of another line of Auden's: "Always the soft idiot softly *me*.")

Once one becomes God's lover, however, one can no longer be completely enclosed in oneself, but one cannot escape that fate simply by returning God's love—at least not if returning that love is conceived of merely as a passion of the soul. To return God's love properly involves *imitatio dei*—"Be thou holy, for I the lord thy God am holy." I have to understand that the very fact that God is able to love a person like myself, to love freely, should inspire me to love my neighbor. In agreement with all traditional Jewish teaching, Rosenzweig insists that love of God cannot have a, so to speak, "vertical dimension" without a "horizontal dimension"; "love of God" without a direction out to other fellow human beings is not really love of God at all. My love of God must enable me to see how isolated I was, and must allow me to break out of that isolation by loving my neighbor. But what is it to love one's neighbor?

LOVE OF ONE'S NEIGHBOR

When Rosenzweig holds that it is only by being awakened to the fact that I am loved by someone wholly Other that I can learn to love my neighbor, he is not denying that one can be involved with other human beings, help other human beings, love other human beings—that is, *particular* other human beings—without a God-relation. But, like Levinas—and Levinas testifies repeatedly to the extent to which he was inspired by reading Rosenzweig—he believes that meaningful love of the other, the love that makes one (in Levinas's words, not Rosenzweig's) "a human being worthy of the name," cannot be a selective love. It is not enough to love my friends; I have to be able to love human beings who are not "attractive," who do not "appeal to me." I have to be able to love each and every human being as a human being.

That means that I have to be able, in Rosenzweig's language, to love the "nighest" [*der Nächste*], the one who is closest to me, no matter who the "nighest" turns out to be. But there are differences as well as similarities between Levinas and Rosenzweig.

For Rosenzweig, the awareness of being loved by a personal God arrives in some sense *prior to* my hearing the command to love the nighest,[15] while for Levinas, as we shall see, the reverse is the case. In Rosenzweig's phenomenology, it is the awareness of God's love that evokes in the beloved the desire to be worthy of that love— fundamentally, by *imitating* it, by showing love to "the nighest."

ROSENZWEIG'S NOTION OF REDEMPTION

To complete our discussion, we must take note of Rosenzweig's notion of redemption. The aspiration for "matrimony" between God and the individual soul does not terminate with the individual soul's taking up the ethical task of loving the "nighest." Judaism is a communal religion. Jews are supposed to pray in groups of at least ten (ten males, in the Orthodox tradition). And Rosenzweig is constantly concerned with the whole Jewish people as God's chosen people (although Christians are also in a sense a "chosen people"—chosen to bring the "pagans" into the light of monotheism). My love of God and my love of my neighbor are not supposed to stop there; rather, they are supposed to lead me to envisage *redemption*. And here I need to mention a surprising aspect of Rosenzweig's theology. Up to now I have stressed the nontraditional character of that theology—for example, Rosenzweig's relaxed attitude to the question of the veracity of particular biblical stories, and his reinterpretation of the doctrine that revelation was a historic event, so that the original "revelation" was not the event, if it occurred, of Moses receiving the Torah on Mount Sinai, but goes, so to speak, all the way back to Adam. This might lead one to expect that redemption would be "philosophically" reinterpreted by Rosenzweig as well, perhaps as something that should always aspire to, or, as something we approach asymptotically but never actually achieve. But Rosenzweig explicitly rejects this idea, in a passage in which he describes the Islamic *ijma* as an analogue of the modern conception of progress. He criticizes both as conceptions, not of the messianic future which one expects at every moment, but of the infinitely extended and projected past:

> Even if there is talk of "eternal" progress—in truth it is but "interminable" progress that is meant. It is a progress which progresses permanently on its way, where every moment has the guaranteed assurance that its turn will yet come, where it can thus be as certain of its coming into existence as a transpired moment of its already being-in-existence. Thus the real idea of progress resists nothing so strongly as the idea that the "ideal goal" could and should be reached, perhaps in the next moment, or even this very moment. The believer in the kingdom uses the term "progress" only to employ the jargon of his time; in reality he means the kingdom. It is the veritable shibboleth for distinguishing him from the authentic devotee of progress whether he does not resist the prospect and duty of anticipating the "goal" at the very next moment. The future is no future without this anticipation and the inner compulsion for it, without this "wish to bring about the Messiah before his time" and the temptation to "coerce the kingdom of God into being"; without these, it is only a past distended endlessly and projected forward. For without such anticipation, the moment is not eternal; it is something that drags itself everlastingly along the long, long trail of time.[16]

Rosenzweig's belief that the world will be redeemed at some future point, that there will be an eschatological redemption—and he insists that this belief is essential to Jewish faith—does not mean that he claims to be able to describe what the redeemed state of the world will be beyond the conception that it will be a state in which the love of God and the love of the neighbor are truly universalized. As he puts it in a letter to the Reform Rabbi Benno Jacob included in *Franz Rosenzweig: His Life and Thought*:

> I find myself unable to formulate just how I think the messianic future will be. But that is no proof against it. When the time comes, the details will fall into place. I am not naïve enough to fancy that peace among peoples and groups can come about without a radical change in human nature, a change which contemplated from the present must appear in the light of a miracle. That I do have faith in that future I owe to our Prayer Book. I cannot exclude Zion from this faith. Just how great, how Jewish, how "modern," a Palestine will be grouped around it, I do not know. But when the time comes I am sure I will not be disturbed by the fact that this Zion—not a heavenly but a messianic and hence earthly Zion—will be surrounded by what is "modern" in the sense of the time, no more than I am disturbed by the paraphernalia of the 'history of civilization' which is grouped about my mental image of biblical antiquity; but also no more than I begrudge the Palestine of today its factories and automobile roads. It belongs! (355)

But redemption is not simply something that Rosenzweig believes will happen in the future. Central to Rosenzweig's whole theology, his whole picture of the life of the ideal Jew is the concept that he or she experiences redemption as something both future *and* present now; that is to say, he or she *anticipates* the future redemption so strongly that it virtually is happening now. He or she experiences redemption as *simultaneously* "present," as "something that might happen in the next moment," *and* as something that will happen in the distant future.

When Rosenzweig tells us that he experiences redemption in this way, he is not contradicting himself, any more than lovers would be if they were to tell us that they experience their love for each other in one way as completely fulfilled, in another way as something whose fulfillment they hope to enjoy in the immediate future, and yet again as something whose fulfillment they expect to experience over the course of their whole lives. Just as religious people are not contradicting themselves (and here I am borrowing an example from Wittgenstein) if they speaks of the "eye of God" without supposing for one moment that God has *eyebrows,* so, I think, Rosenzweig is not contradicting himself by describing redemption as simultaneously present and future.

JEWS AND REDEMPTION

As we mentioned in chapter 1, Jews have a special place in Rosenzweig's thought—a world-historic place, or perhaps one should say a "world-ahistoric place," since their special destiny is supposed to be to stand outside history. The point, so to speak, of the eternal existence of Jews—and for Rosenzweig that means the eternal existence of the Diaspora[17]—is to be a sort of here-and-now model of how the redeemed state of humanity might look. Jews are supposed to be content and fulfilled in living Godly lives, lives which, as it were, are already redeemed, and therefore do not have to be redeemed by the Christian Church. And Rosenzweig writes movingly both in the *Star* and, more briefly, in *Understanding the Sick and the Healthy,* of the way in which the Jewish liturgical calendar and the Daily Prayer Book and the Sabbath and the doing of *mitzvot* can produce the sense that he talks about of being already redeemed and anticipating redemption, in the double sense of expecting it at any moment and anticipating it as a distant eschatological event.

Speaking now for myself, I can imagine the complex experience to which Rosenzweig refers, but I believe that it is something that can be experienced by a community of faith within any religious tradition that anticipates or hopes for ultimate redemption, at least when that community is a truly spiritual one. In Rosenzweig's rather peculiar view of world history, the Christian exists simply to go out and convert all the "pagans." But the average Christian is not a missionary—it has not been the case for millennia that most Christians are missionaries—and indeed the fact that a community of Muslims or a community of Zen Buddhists could also exhibit the features that Rosenzweig values is something that he excludes from his intellectual field of vision at a considerable cost—the cost of contempt for religions other than the valorized two that seems strange in someone who shows himself, in his life and in so much of his writing, to have been such an attractive spirit. Fortunately, even his contempt for paganism and religions other than Christianity and Judaism is *not* a contempt for the religious life of the followers of those religions, or a claim for the superiority of the religious life of the individual Jew or Christian. As Rosenzweig states in "The New Thinking":

> By right have the temples of the gods crumbled, by right do their statues stand in museums, their services, insofar as they were ordered and regulated, may have been a singularly monstrous error—yet the prayer which rose to [these gods] from a tormented heart, and the tears shed by the Carthaginian father who led his son to Moloch sacrifice—these cannot have been unheard and could not have remained unseen. Or should God have waited for Mount Sinai, or even Golgotha? No, as

little as paths lead from Sinai or from Golgotha, on which He can be reached with certainty, so little can He have denied Himself [the possibility of] encountering even the person who sought Him on the trails around Olympus. There is no temple built that would be so near to him that man might take comfort from that proximity, nor is there one so distant from him that His arm could not easily reach even there. There is no direction from which He could not come and none from which He had to come; there is no block of wood in which He may not take up his dwelling, and no psalm of David that always reaches his ear. (130)

To sum up: the whole purpose of human life is revelation, and the whole content of revelation is love. The love between the Lover and the Beloved culminates in "matrimony," that is, redemption. And redemption has a personal aspect—it is something experienced by each religious person; a communal aspect—it is something exemplified and modeled by the Jewish religious community as whole; and it has an eschatological dimension, but it is not only eschatological because its future occurrence is something that is "present" to the individual Jew *now*.[18]

3 | What

I and Thou

Is Really Saying

In *Israelis and the Jewish Tradition*, David Hartman speaks of the disastrous psychological burden of what he calls "event-grounded theology":

> The Six-Day War taught me that a deep part of me agreed with certain features of [Yehudah] Halevi's[1] understanding of Judaism. Nevertheless, I also vividly recall the extreme emotional change from the elation over the victory to the despair and anxiety that gripped the country during and after the Yom Kippur war. Although I still acknowledged the power of events, I now recognize the manic-depressive consequences possible in an event-grounded theology. I am drawn to the sobriety of Maimonides and the Talmudic tradition as ways of moderating the event-driven passions of traumatic historical events.[2]

If one has ever read the major prophets, Isaiah, Jeremiah, and Ezekiel, and then the twelve so-called "minor prophets" through in succession, one knows just how intensely the problem Hartman is wrestling with was felt by all of them. For biblical Judaism—Judaism before the sages of the Talmud (let alone the philosophers)—bad things were supposed to happen to bad people (or peoples—there is considerable wavering in the Jewish Bible between the idea that an angry God will punish a whole people and the thought that he will spare righteous individuals), and the oscillation between optimism and despair produced by the experiences of the Assyrian and Babylonian captivities is palpable in the prophetic writings. Perhaps the most moving lines in that most tragic of books, Eikha (Lamentations) are these: "We have transgressed and rebelled; you have not pardoned. You have covered yourself with anger and pursued us; you have slain us without pity. You have covered yourself with a cloud so that prayer should not pass through." (Lam. 3:42–44)

Already in Psalms the stance of blaming all the bad things that happen to us on our own wrong-doing is sometimes rejected. Thus in Psalm 44 (12–20) we find: "You have given us like sheep to be eaten, and have scattered us among the nations. You sell your people for no great profit, and have not set a high price on them. You make us a taunt to our neighbors, a scorn and a derision to those round about us. You make us a byword among the nations, a shaking of the head among the peoples. . . . all this is come upon us; yet we have not forgotten you, nor have we been false to your covenant. Our heart is not turned back, nor have our steps declined from your way, although you have sore broken us in the place of jackals, and covered us with the shadow of death."

When it becomes impossible to explain all the bad things that happen to us as our own fault—morally as well as psychology impossible—as it seems to have been impos-

sible for the author of these lines, then one has to search
for a theology that is less guilt-ridden than the Judaism
that the prophets seem to be assuming, or, if one is Orthodox (as I am not) one has to reinterpret what the prophets
say. Such a search, and such reinterpretations, are present
already in the Talmud. For example, instead of teaching
that God rewards and punishes peoples in historic time,
the sages of the Talmud pictured a God who defers justice
to eschatological time:

> Why were they called men of the Great Assembly? Because
> they restored the crown of the divine attributes to its ancient
> completeness. Moses had come and said, 'The great, mighty,
> and the awesome God.' [Deut. 10:17] Then Jeremiah came
> and said, 'Aliens are frolicking in his temple; where then are
> His awesome deeds?' Hence he omitted the word 'awesome'
> [in Jer. 32:18]. Daniel came and said: 'Aliens are enslaving
> his sons; where are his mighty deeds?' Hence he omitted the
> word 'mighty' [in Dan. 9:4]. But they came and said, 'On the
> contrary! Therein lie His mighty deeds that he suppresses His
> wrath, that He extends long-suffering to the wicked. Therein
> lie His awesome powers; for but for fear of Him, how could one
> nation persist among the [many] nations?' [*b. Yoma* 69b]

While agreeing with the sages of the Talmud that we
should not expect secular reward for our virtues and good
deeds, or punishment for vices and wicked deeds (either
for our own or those of other people), and that "the reward of a mitzvah is a mitzvah," Jewish philosophers have
never been able to rest content with these passages; as
philosophers, it goes without saying that they sought and
still seek a more philosophical account. Maimonides, for
example, reinterpreted the horrifying punishments that
the prophets and Lamentations describe in terms of in-
telligible social causation; a nation that violates halakhic

law, including moral law, will be unstable, and this instability (and the greed and folly that produce the instability)
will result in foreign and domestic conflicts that will end
by bringing disaster on that nation. To say that God pun-
ished the Jewish people for idolatry, greed, oppression of
the poor, and so on, is thus just a way of saying, in pic-
turesque terms that the masses can understand, that im-
morality results in disaster.[3] In this book, however, I shall
not attempt to describe the philosophy of Maimonides. Instead, in this chapter I want to describe the ways in which
one of the greatest Jewish philosophers of the last hundred
years, Martin Buber (like that other great Jewish philosopher, Emmanuel Levinas, whose views I describe in chapter 4) tried to produce a conception of our relation to God
that does not so much "solve" the problem of Evil, as try
to keep it from even being formulated. (They are not the
same; Levinas and Buber certainly have disagreements,
but I am certain that we can be enriched by reflecting on
them.) What I shall say in this chapter is simply an attempt to explain Buber's views.

Martin Buber

Very often people are surprised that I value the thought of
Martin Buber. There is an idea around that he was a "light-
weight," someone not as profound or original as Levinas
or Rosenzweig. Not surprisingly, I find this idea voiced by
people who have not read a line of Buber's masterpiece,
I and Thou, as well as by people who have read that work
superficially.[4] I shall begin my account of what I am calling Buber's "theology" with some reflections on the possible reasons for this negative impression.

It may be that two factors are at work. Buber purports
to teach us something about relationship, including relationship to other people (notice: I did not say *especially*,

relationships to other people), and many people find the idea of being told something *normative* about relations to others (as opposed to something "statistical," or something psychoanalytic, or something political or in any way social-scientific) embarrassing, perhaps even offensive. If Levinas, who is explicitly doing this very thing, does not evoke a similar reaction, that may be because those who value Levinas imagine they are reading a "postmodern" writer, and thus someone who is *nouvelle vague.*

Both in this chapter and the next, I shall employ a concept I take from Stanley Cavell, the concept of *moral perfectionism.*[5] Moral perfectionists believe that the ancient questions, "Am I living as I am supposed to live?"; "Is my life something more than vanity, or worse, mere conformity?"; "Am I making the best effort I can to reach [in Cavellian language] my unattained but attainable self?" make all the difference in the world. Emerson, Nietzsche, and Mill are three of Cavell's principle examples. (Cavell also detects perfectionist strains in Rousseau and in Kant.)

When Emerson and Mill attack "conformity," what they object to are not the *principles* to which the conformist pays lip service. What Emerson and Mill tell us is that if conformity is all that one's allegiance comes to, then even the best principles are *useless.* Such a philosopher is a "perfectionist" because she or he always describes the commitment we ought to have in ways that seem impossibly demanding; but such a philosopher is also a realist, because s/he realizes that it is only by keeping an "impossible" demand in view that one can strive for one's "unattained but attainable self."

Every one of the great Jewish philosophers, including the great twentieth-century Jewish thinkers (particularly Buber, Cohen, Levinas, and Rosenzweig), was a moral perfectionist in this sense. The famous "I-Thou" in Buber is a relation that Buber believes is *demanded* of us, and without which no system of moral rules and no institution can have any real value. For Levinas there is a different "I-Thou" relation, one that is more important than Buber's I-Thou,[6] and for Rosenzweig, as we have seen, there is a complex system of such relations to man, to the world, and to God. But one cannot understand any of these relations without understanding this "perfectionist" dimension.

"Moral perfectionists" *do* embarrass as well as inspire us, and that is why we are always ambivalent about them. (It is why many philosophers are ambivalent about Cavell himself.) In Buber's case there is an additional problem, and that is the failure of many readers (especially those who give up on him without much reflection) to see that his thought is not as simple and transparent as may appear at first blush. Indeed, although Buber does not refer to a vast amount of philosophical literature in the way in which Levinas does, his thought is no less complex, and if one refuses a priori to believe that this might be the case, one will never be able to grasp what Buber is really saying.

Precisely because both Buber and Levinas are complex thinkers, it would be foolish on my part to pretend that I can explain the philosophy of even one of them "standing on one foot."[7] What I hope to do, however, is not merely to share my enthusiasm for the work and perhaps stimulate others to read it, although I certainly want to do at least that. My greater aim is to provide guidance on what to look out for and what mistakes to avoid. In Buber's case, because he is so often misunderstood, I shall concentrate on this negative task.

THE "I-YOU" RELATION

Before I do that, however, let us review what most people know about *I and Thou*. Everyone who has read Buber's

classic book, and many who have merely glanced at it, or
not even that, know that it contains a normative account
of human relations, an attempt to describe an ideal type
of relation, the "I-You" relation. Walter Kaufman rightly
pointed out that the German *"Du"* in the title *Ich und Du*
is simply the pronoun one uses in talking to friends and
family, and that translating it by the now archaic "thou"
already falsifies Buber's thought by making it somehow
fake-solemn (although he kept the "Thou" in the title of
his translation, doubtless because the work was so well
known by that title, while eliminating all the *thous* from
the body of the work). Indeed, the use of *thou* has pretty
much disappeared in recent translations of the Bible, for
the same reason. (When the traditional Jew addresses God
as *atah*, "you," and we translate this as "thou," we lose sight
of the fact that we are supposed to address God just as we
address a friend or a parent or a child, and not to use a special form of address reserved only for God.) Kaufman's decision to translate *Du* as "you" in the body of the text already removes the first stumbling block in the path of the
reader of Buber's book.

[Another stumbling block, for the English reader, is the
lack of an adequate footnote explaining the sense of the peculiar expression "spiritual beings" (*geistige Wesenheiten*)—
that occurs in the first few pages of the work. To an English reader, "spiritual beings" suggest *angels*, if it suggests
anything, but what Buber means are intellectual and aesthetic forms and not angels. A paradigm case of what he
envisions would be a concept for a work of art, a concept
that a musician or a painter or a poet or any other sort of
artist devotes selfless attention to, attention uncorrupted
by self-interest or desire for "success," in her effort to bring
the concept into successful realization. This example of
an "I-You" relation brings out the way in which there is a
quasi-*aesthetic* (as well as a quasi-religious) dimension in

all genuine "I-You" relations, but the clumsy translation (even Kaufman, surprisingly, is guilty here!) obscures the intention.]

Secondly, every reader knows that Buber contrasted the "I-You" relation to another relation, the "I-It" relation. But already at this point two important misunderstandings lurk!

First misunderstanding: Buber thinks the "I-You" relation is always good; the "I-It" relation is always bad. This is doubly wrong. The "I-You" relation has a number of characteristics, among which are its exclusiveness-at-the-moment (*except* in the case of the most important "I-You" relation, the "I-You" relation to God, in which all of one's other "I-You" relations are supposed to be taken up) and the fact that the You is experienced as an organic unity rather than as an object to be used or analyzed. But whether a particular "I-You" relation is *good* depends on the appropriateness of the object, and Buber points out (in a passage that many readers seem not to *see*) that there can be a *demonic* "I-You" relation. Interestingly—and this was not a reaction to the Holocaust, because *I and Thou* was written between 1919 and 1922—Buber's example of such a relation is a relation to a *dictator* (Napoleon).[8]

Buber also emphasizes that the "I-It" relation is not always bad, and I do not accuse most readers of overlooking this, but, if my own students are representative readers, they tend to regard this as a sort of grudging concession to the demands of everyday life. This is not just a misreading of one or two passages; *it literally misses the point of the entire book.* But to explain why, I have to point out one somewhat subtle feature of Buber's text: there is, within the text, not only talk of an "I-It" relation, but also talk of an "It-world."[9] Why this is important will, I hope, become clear shortly.

If Buber really thought that the *telos* of a fully human life was to achieve and *remain in* an "I-You" relation (whether to God or to a human person or persons), then his criticism of Buddhism would apply to himself as well. According to Buber, the mistake of Buddhist doctrine is precisely to think that the *telos* is to stay in a state that takes one outside the normal world (I am not going to discuss whether this is or is not a misinterpretation of Buddhism—I suspect it applies to some forms of Buddhism and not to others). Buber's "I-You" relation is one that can only be of short duration, but its significance is that after one has had an "I-You" relation with the divine, the "It-World" is transformed. There are, so to speak, two sorts of "I-It" relations: *mere* "I-It" relations and *transformed* "I-It" relations.

Observe the following statements: "The It-world can be transfigured to the point where it confronts and represents the You" (99); "By virtue of [pure relationship] the You-world has the power to give form; the spirit can permeate the It-world and change it" (149). The thought is that the end of the You encounter need not mean lapsing back into the purely instrumental I-It attitude; it can mean serving the eternal You within the It-world: "Whoever goes forth in truth to the world goes forth to God" (143). "As we have nothing but a You on our lips when we enter the encounter, it is with this on our lips that we are *released into the world*" (159, emphasis added).

Moreover, the transformation that Buber envisages is not just a transformation of the individual's life, although that is where transformation always begins, but also the transformation of our social life. One of my favorite passages in *I and Thou* is the passage in which Buber replies to an interlocutor who thinks this is all head-in-the-clouds rubbish, and that what we need instead is the "know-how" of the practically minded leader of the political-economic machine (i.e., economics and Realpolitik):

> Speaker, you speak too late. But a moment ago you might have believed your own speech; now this is no longer possible. For an instant you saw no less than I that the state is no longer led . . . the leaders merely *seem* to rule the racing engines. And in this instant while you speak, you can hear as well as I how the machinery of the economy is beginning to hum in an unwonted manner; the overseers give you a superior smile, but death lurks in their hearts. They tell you that they have adjusted the apparatus to modern conditions, but you notice that henceforth they can only adjust themselves to the apparatus, as long as that permits it. Their spokesmen instruct you that the economy is taking over the heritage of the state; you know that there is nothing to be inherited but the despotism of the proliferating It under which the I, more and more impotent, is still dreaming that it is in command. (*I and Thou*, 97)

In sum, the aim of Buberian philosophy is to teach us that the experience of the divine is not an end in itself—but let me put the stress in the right place—the *experience* of the divine is not an end in itself, and the "I-You" relation is not an end in itself, but rather the end is the *transformation* of life *in* the world, life in the *It-world*, through the transforming effect of the recurrent "I-You" relation.

Second misunderstanding: all that is important in I and Thou *is the teaching about personal relationships; all that stuff about God can be ignored.* While Buber's phenomenology of personal relationships, or rather of the "I-You" moment in a personal relationship, is moving and insightful, it is not, I think, where Buber's true originality lies. For example, although no one, to my knowledge, has previously thought to compare G. E. Moore (the founder, along with Bertrand Russell, of the English school of analytic philosophy) with Martin Buber, the account of friendship in Moore's *Prin-*

cipia Ethica does in certain respects anticipate Buber's account of the "I-You" relation.[10] Indeed, it is precisely that account of ideal friendship that especially moved the members of the Bloomsbury Group. (A wonderful description of Moore, the group, and the moral impact of Moore's teaching is contained in John Maynard Keynes's lovely memoir "My Early Beliefs.")[11] In particular, the similarity between the appreciation of the friend and the best kind of aesthetic appreciation is noted by Moore, as it is by Buber. But Moore is an atheist, for whom ideal friendship is simply a good thing—a good "organic unity" which is, at the same time, a part of the organic unity that constitutes the total world whose goodness the members of the Bloomsbury Group were constantly trying to estimate,[12] while for Buber the "I-You" relation to the friend points *beyond* the friendship, points to and ideally leads to the relation to the divine, to the ultimate You.

It is, I think, in his theology that Buber is truly original. That theology can be fairly briefly stated, although an elucidation of the brief statement I shall attempt could take volumes. My brief statement (in my words, not Buber's) consists of two claims:

(1) It is impossible to describe God, or to theorize about him. Indeed, the very attempt causes one to miss the target entirely.

(2) What one can do is speak *to* God, or rather, to enter into an "I-You" relation with God, a relation in which all the partial "I-You" relations (to people, to "Geistliche Wesen," to trees and animals, and other natural things) are bound up and fulfilled without being obliterated.

Although Buber does not address the so-called "problem of evil" in *I and Thou*, I believe that he offers a truly radical alternative to the "event-driven" and guilt-ridden theology that I referred to at the beginning of this chapter. If one is troubled by the evil in the world, Buber is telling us, one can certainly speak *to* God about it—the Jewish tradition of "wrestling with God" (this is the literal meaning of the word *Israel*) is fully consonant with the Buberian spirit—and the psalmist who wrote the lines that I quoted earlier ("Our heart is not turned back, nor have our steps declined from your way, although you have sore broken us in the place of jackals, and covered us with the shadow of death") was not *theorizing* about the problem of evil but speaking to God about it from within an "I-You" relation.

Note that Buber's theology is neither "negative" theology nor "positive theology" in the traditional sense. For the traditional negative theologian, for example Maimonides, the impossibility of theorizing about God is itself the product of theory ("speculation," in the traditional metaphysical sense). And addressing God as if God were a person is a metaphysical mistake. For the traditional positive theologian, God is *literally* a person, and we can *describe* what sort of person God is. But for Buber the whole enterprise of metaphysical "speculation" is a mistake, even if (in its "negative" form) what it leads to is a recognition of the impossibility of capturing God by means of metaphysical speculation.

Not only is the idea of theorizing about God rejected by Buber, but so also is the idea of *a theory of religious knowledge,* an answer to the question, "How do you know that God exists?" To ask that question is to stand outside of relationship. For Buber, one comes to God by entering into relationship with God, and an I-You relation is never a matter of *knowledge.* Thus, when Buber writes about the impossibility of describing or theorizing about God, he is not engaged in "negative theology," as one might at first suppose; his sentences are hortatory, not descriptive, and they are meant to suggest, to point, to invite to a certain mode of being in the world, not to prove or demonstrate. The idea is that if one achieves that mode of being in the world, however briefly—and it is not a mode of being one can stay in long but rather a mode that one can reenter at different points in one's life—then, ideally, that mode of being—the relation to the ultimate You—will *transform* one's life even when one is back in the "It world." Moreover—and this is the connection between Buber's theology and his many-sided social concerns—Buber believes that all genuine community, and all genuine moments of transformation in history, require something like a *shared* relation to the ultimate You. All purely materialistic "solutions" to the world's problems, whether they valorize socialism (Marx's "historical materialism") or capitalism (our contemporary worship of "the free market") must fail without such a moment of relationship. If Buber's Zionism involved a lifelong concern with the rights and aspirations of the Palestinians, as it did, it was because for him an immoral Zionism was a doomed Zionism.

4 | Levinas on What Is Demanded of Us

Levinas survived the Second World War under difficult and humiliating circumstances,[1] while his family, with the exception of his wife and daughter, perished. These experiences may well have shaped Levinas's sense that what is demanded of us is an "infinite" willingness to be available to and for the other's suffering. "The Other's hunger—be it of the flesh, or of bread—is sacred; only the hunger of the third party limits its rights," Levinas states in the preface to *Difficult Freedom*. To understand fully what Levinas means here would be to understand his whole philosophy. I want to attempt a beginning at such an understanding.

LEVINAS'S MISSION TO THE GENTILES

Levinas's audience is typically a gentile audience; he celebrates Jewish particularity in essays addressed to Christians and to modern people generally. Levinas is fully aware of this. Thus he writes (in "A Religion for Adults," 13), "Lest the union between men of goodwill which I desire to see be brought about only in a vague and abstract mode, I wish to insist here on the particular routes open to Jewish monotheism." A few pages later, he writes:

> A truth is universal when it applies to every reasonable being. A religion is universal when it is open to all. In this sense the Judaism that links the Divine to the moral has always aspired to be universal. But the revelation of morality, which discovers a human society, also discovers the place of election, which in this universal society, returns to the person who receives this revelation. This election is made up not of privileges but of responsibilities. It is a nobility based not on author's rights [*droit d'auteur*] or on a birthright [*droit d'aînesse*] conferred by a divine caprice, but on the position of each human I [*moi*] . . . The basic intuition of moral growing-up perhaps consists in perceiving that I am not *the equal* of the Other. This applies in a very strict sense: I see myself *obligated* with respect to the Other; consequently I am infinitely more demanding of myself than of others . . . This "position outside nations" of which the Pentateuch speaks is realized in the concept of Israel and its particularism. It is a particularism that conditions universality, *and it is a moral category rather than a historical fact to do with Israel* [my emphasis—HP]. (21–22)

In this passage Levinas reinterprets the doctrine of the election of Israel in terms of his own ethics–phenomenology, so that it becomes a "particularism that conditions universality"—becomes, that is, the asymmetry that Levinas everywhere insists on between what I require of myself and what I am entitled to require of anyone else; and he tells us that so reinterpreted, election "is a universal moral category rather than a historical fact to do with Israel." Here and elsewhere, Levinas universalizes Judaism. To understand him, one has to understand the paradoxical claim implicit in his writing that, in essence, *all human beings are Jews.*

In one place, we see this universalization of the category of *Jew* connected with Levinas's own losses in the Holocaust. The dedication page to *Otherwise than Being or Beyond Essence* bears two dedications. The upper one is in French and reads (in translation), "*To the memory of those who were closest among the six million assassinated by the National Socialists, and of the millions and millions of all confessions and all nations, victims of the same hatred of the other man, the same antisemitism.*"

The other dedication is in Hebrew, and using traditional phraseology, it dedicates the volume to the memories of his father, mother, brother, father-in-law, and mother-in-law. What is most striking about this page is the way in which Levinas dedicates the book to the memory of "those closest" (to himself), and simultaneously identifies all victims of the same "hatred of the other man," regardless of their nation and religious affiliation, as victims of *antisemitism*.

ETHICS AS FIRST PHILOSOPHY

Levinas is famous for the claim that ethics is *first philosophy*[2] —by which he means not only that ethics must not be derived from any metaphysics, not even an "ontic" metaphysics (i.e., an "antiontological" antimetaphysics) like Heidegger's, but also that all thinking about what it is to be a human being must *begin* with such an "ungrounded" ethics. This does not mean that Levinas wishes to deny the validity of, for example, the "Categorical Imperative." What he rejects is any formula of the form "Behave in such and such a way *because. . . .*" In many different ways, Levinas tell us that it is a disaster to say "treat the other as an end and not as a means *because. . . .*"[3]

Yet to most people there seems to be an obvious "because." If you ask someone, "Why *should we* act so that we could will the maxims of our actions as universal laws?" or "Why should we treat the humanity in others always as an end and never as a mere means?" or "Why *should we* attempt to relieve the suffering of others?" ninety-nine times out of a hundred the answer will be, "Because the other is fundamentally the same as you." The thought—or rather the cliché—is that if I realized how much the other is *like* me I would automatically feel a desire to help. But the limitations of such a "grounding" of ethics only have to be mentioned to become obvious.

The danger in grounding ethics in the idea that we are all "fundamentally the same" is that a door is opened for a Holocaust. One only has to believe that some people are not "really" the same, to destroy all the force of such a grounding. Nor is there only the danger of a denial of our common humanity (the Nazis claimed that Jews were vermin in superficially human form!). Every good novelist rubs our noses in the extent of human dissimilarity, and many novels pose the question: "If you really knew what some other people were like, could you feel sympathy with them at all?"

But Kantians will point out that Kant saw this too. *That* is why Kant grounds ethics not in "sympathy" but in our common rationality. But then what becomes of our obligations to those whose rationality we can more or less plausibly deny?

These are *ethical* reasons for refusing to base ethics on either a metaphysical or a psychological "because." Levinas sees metaphysics as an attempt to view the world as a totality, from "outside," as it were.[4] And like Rosenzweig, whom he cites, Levinas believes that the significance that life has for the human subject is lost in such a perspective.[5] Thus Levinas tells Philippe Nemo,

> There have been few protestations in the history of philosophy against this totalization. In what concerns me, it is in Franz Rosenzweig's philosophy, which is essentially a discussion of

> Hegel, that for the first time I encountered a critique of to-
> tality. . . . .In Rosenzweig there is thus an explosion of the to-
> tality and the opening of quite a different route in the search
> for what is reasonable.[6]

Levinas's daring move is to insist that the impossibility
of a metaphysical grounding for ethics shows that there
is something wrong with metaphysics, and not with ethics. But I will defer discussion of Levinas's attitudes to philosophy for the moment.

LEVINAS AS A "MORAL PERFECTIONIST"

It is possible to distinguish two species of moral philosophers. One species, the legislators, provide detailed moral
and political rules. If one is a philosopher of this sort, then
one is likely to think that the whole problem of political
philosophy (for example) would be solved if we could de-
vise a constitution for the Ideal State.

But there are philosophers of another kind, the philosophers whom (using a term we owe to Stanley Cavell)
we called "moral perfectionists" in chapter 3. It is not,
Cavell hastens to tell us, that the perfectionists deny the
value of what the legislative philosophers are attempting
to do; it is that they believe there is need for something
prior to principles or a constitution, without which the
best principles and the best constitution are worthless.[7]

As we explained in chapter 3, what moral perfectionists tell us is that if conformity is all one's allegiance to
one's principles comes to, then even the best principles
are *useless*. As I said there, these philosophers are "perfectionists" because they always describe the commitment we
ought to have in ways that seem impossibly demanding;
but they are also realists, because they realize that it is only
by keeping an "impossible" demand in view that one can
strive for one's "unattained but attainable self."

For Levinas, the distinction between the legislative moment and the perfectionist moment in ethics is also a distinction of tasks: Levinas sees *his* task as describing the fundamental obligation to the other.[8] The further task of proposing moral/political rules belongs to a later stage, the stage of "justice," and while Levinas tells us how and why there are two stages, it is not his task to write a textbook of ethics like Rawls's *A Theory of Justice*. Almost always in Levinas's writing the term *ethics* refers to what I have called the moral perfectionist moment, the moment when he describes what I just called "the fundamental obligation."

THE FUNDAMENTAL OBLIGATION

Consider the question, "Imagine you were in a situation in which your obligations to others did not conflict with focusing entirely on one other human being. What sort of attitude, what sort of relation, should you strive for towards that other?" Like Buber, Levinas believes *this* is the fundamental question that must be addressed, that must be answered before discussing the complications that arise when one has to consider the conflicting demands of a number of others (when what Levinas calls "the hunger of the third party" limits the demands of the Other), or even the complications that arise when you consider that you yourself are an "other" to others. To describe Levinas's answer in full would require a description of his entire philosophy. (In particular, one would have to describe the puzzling notion of "infinite responsibility.") For now I shall focus on two elements:

(1) The first element is best explained by a Hebrew word: *hineni*. The word is a combination of two elements: "hine" (pronounced *hiné*) and "ni," a contraction of the pronoun "ani," I). "Hine" is often translated "behold," but there is no reference to *seeing* in the root meaning. It might

be translated as "here," but unlike the Hebrew synonyms for "here," "kan" and "po," it cannot occur in a mere descriptive proposition. "Hine" is used *only presentationally;* that is, I can say "hine hameil," *here is the coat,* when I point to the coat (hence the translation: "Behold the coat!"), but I cannot say, "Etmol hameil haya hine" (Yesterday the coat was *hine*) to mean "Yesterday the coat was here"; I have to say "Etmol hameil haya po" or "Etmol ha meil haya kan." Thus *hine* performs the speech-act of calling attention to, or *presenting,* not describing. *Hine hameil!* performs the speech act of presenting the coat (*meil*) and thus "hineni!" performs the speech act of *presenting myself,* the speech act of *making myself available to another.*

The places in which *hineni* is used in this way in the Jewish Bible are highly significant. The most tremendous of these occurs at the beginning of Genesis 22 which tells the story of the Binding of Isaac. "And it came to pass after these things that God did test Abraham, and said to him Abraham: and he said *hineni*" (22:1). Note that here Abraham is offering himself to God *unreservedly.* (That Abraham also says *hineni* to Isaac in 22:7 is an essential part of the paradox of this text.)

When Levinas speaks of saying *me voici!*[9] what he means is virtually unintelligible if one is not aware of the biblical resonance. *The fundamental obligation we have, Levinas is telling us, is the obligation to make ourselves available to the neediness (and especially the suffering) of the other person.* I am commanded to say *hineni!* to the Other (and to do so without reservation, just as Abraham's *hineni* to God was without reservation) and this does *not* presuppose that I sympathize with the other, and certainly does not presuppose (what Levinas regards as the self-aggrandizing gesture) of claiming to "understand" the other. Levinas insists that the closer I come to another by all ordinary standards of closeness (especially, for example, in a love relationship),[10] the more I am required to be aware of my distance from grasping the other's essential reality, and the more I am required to respect that distance. As I have already said, this fundamental obligation is a "perfectionist" one, not a code of behavior or a theory of justice. But, Levinas believes, if the taking on of this fundamental obligation is not present, then the best code of behavior or the best theory of justice will not help.

In contrast, according to Buber what I should seek is a relation that is *reciprocal*. But Levinas stresses the *asymmetry* of the fundamental moral relation: "I see myself *obligated* with respect to the Other; consequently I am infinitely more demanding of myself than of others." Before reciprocity must come ethics; to seek to base ethics on reciprocity is once again to seek to base it on the illusory "sameness" of the other person.

(2) I have mentioned a fundamental *obligation* in connection with Levinas (and a fundamental *relation* in connection with Buber). The choice of the word *obligation* was deliberate: for Levinas, to be a human being in the normative sense (to be what Jews call a *mensch*) involves recognizing that I am *commanded* to say *hineni*. In Levinas's phenomenology, this means that I am commanded without experiencing a commander (my only experience of the commander is the experience of being commanded), and without either a metaphysical explanation of the nature of the command or a metaphysical justification for the command. If you have to ask, "*Why* should I put myself out for him/her?," you are not yet *human*. This is why Levinas must contradict Heidegger: Heidegger thinks that fully appreciating my own death ("being-toward-death") makes

me a true human being as opposed to a mere member of the "they"; Levinas believes that what is essential is the relation to the other.[11] Again, there is a universalization of a Jewish theme here: just as the traditional Jew finds his dignity in obeying the divine command, so Levinas thinks that every human being should find his or her dignity in the obeying of the fundamental ethical command (which will turn out to be "divine" in the only sense Levinas can allow), the command to say *hineni* to the Other, to say *hineni* with what Levinas calls "infinite" responsibility.

Saying Precedes the Said

The foregoing explains Levinas's puzzling statement that "the saying has to be reached in its existence antecedent to the said."[12] For, if by a "said" we mean the content of a proposition, then when I say *hineni* there is no "said." What I do is *make myself available to the other person;* I do this by uttering a verbal formula, but the content of the verbal formula is immaterial, provided it succeeds in presenting me as one who is available.[13]

Levinas's Philosophical Education

One reason why analytic philosophers find Levinas hard to read is that he takes it for granted that reading Husserl and Heidegger is part of the education any properly trained philosopher must have, just as analytic philosophers presuppose an education that includes reading Russell, Frege, Carnap, and Quine. Certainly there are passages in Levinas's writing that can only be understood against the background of their explicit or implicit references to the writings of these two philosophers. Yet Levinas's thought is strikingly independent. For in the respects that are essential from *Levinas's* point of view, he finds Husserl and Heidegger inadequate. I shall try to explain what Levinas is doing with a minimum of reliance on any prior knowledge of the two great "H"s.

HUSSERL AND LEVINAS

"A minimum" does not mean *zero*, however. But what I shall say about Husserl to illustrate the way in which Levinas breaks with him will refer only to the aspect of Husserl's thought that *ought to be* familiar to analytic philosophers (even if it isn't) because it had great influence on one of the founding fathers of their movement, Rudolf Carnap. (Carnap's *Der Raum* is clearly a Husserlian work, and even the *Aufbau* contains acknowledgements of Husserl's influence—e.g. the striking claim, "This is *epoché* in Husserl's sense.")[14]

Especially in *Ideas*,[15] Husserl portrays the world as in some sense a *construction*.[16] Husserl's notion of construction is not Carnap's, but there is no doubt that the latter saw the *Aufbau* as a way of rectifying Husserl's project with the aid of mathematical logic, just as *Der Raum* was Carnap's way of constructing a "Husserlian" philosophy of space with the aid of mathematical logic.

A problem that arises in both of these philosophies is that even if the construction succeeded in its own terms —even if, *per impossibile,* one were to succeed in (re)-constructing "the world" in terms of the philosopher's ontology—the primitive elements of that ontology are *my own* experiences. And there is something *morally* disturbing about this.

To put the point in terms of Carnap's rather than Husserl's notion of construction, suppose that my friend is a phenomenalist and believes that all I am is a logical construction out of *his* sense-data. Should I feel reassured if he tells me that the relevant sentences about his sense-data (the ones that "translate" all of his beliefs about *me* into the system of the *Aufbau*) have the same "verification conditions" as the beliefs they translate? Am I making a mistake if I find that just isn't good enough?[17]

If his avowals of friendship and concern are avowals of an attitude to his own sense-data, then my friend is *narcissistic*. A genuine ethical relation to another presupposes that you realize that *the other person is an independent reality and not in any way your construction*. Here is one of Levinas's many critical descriptions of Western metaphysics cum epistemology:

> Whatever the abyss that separates the psyche of the ancients from the consciousness of the moderns. . . . the necessity of going back to the beginning, or to consciousness, appears as the proper task of philosophy: return to its island to be shut up there in the simultaneity of the eternal instant, approaching the *mens instanea* of God.[18]

The note of scorn is unmistakable! In contrast, according to Levinas,

> Subjectivity of flesh and blood in matter is not . . . a "mode of self-certainty." The proximity of beings of flesh and blood is not their presence in "flesh and bone," is not the fact that they take form for a look, present an exterior, quiddities, forms, give images, which the eye absorbs (and whose alterity the hand that touches or holds suspends easily or lightly, annulling it by the simple grasp, as though no one contested this appropriation.) Nor are material beings reducible to the resistance they oppose to the effort they solicit. [Think of a logical positivist "analysis" of the sentence "A man is in front of me"!] Subjectivity of flesh and blood in matter . . . the-one-for-the-other itself—is the preoriginal signifyingness that gives sense, because it gives.[19]

DESCARTES'S PROOF OF GOD'S EXISTENCE

The significance that the independence of the Other (*l'autrui*) has for Levinas is perhaps best brought out by looking at Levinas's interpretation of Descartes's proof of the existence of God in the Third Meditation.[20] There, Descartes argued that the "infinity" involved in the idea of God could not have been so much as *conceived* of by his mind by means of its own unaided powers, but could only have been put into his mind by God Himself.[21]

If this appears to be an outrageous fallacy to a philosopher, one reason is likely to be that the philosopher thinks of "infinite" as having the meaning it has such statements as "there are infinitely many prime numbers." But this is not what Descartes means at all. Rather, as Kant also saw, to speak of God as "infinitely wise" or "infinitely great" is not to speak mathematically at all.[22]

What then is it to do? Descartes is conventionally thought to have invoked the existence of God because his argument "ran into trouble." But Levinas believes that what Descartes is reporting is not a step in a deductive reasoning, but a profound religious experience, an experience that might be described as an experience of a *fissure*, of a confrontation with something that disrupts all his categories. On this reading, Descartes is not so much proving something as *acknowledging* something, acknowledging a Reality that he could not have constructed, a Reality that *proves its own existence* by the very fact that its presence in my mind turns out to be a *phenomenological impossibility.*

It is not that Levinas *accepts* Descartes's argument, so interpreted. The significance is rather that Levinas *transforms* the argument by substituting the Other for God. So transformed, the "proof" becomes: I know the Other [*l'autrui*] is not part of my "construction of the world" because my encounter with the other is an encounter with a *fissure*, with a being who breaks my categories.

The analogy between Levinas's account of what he calls "a direct relation with the Other"[23] and Descartes's account of his relation to God extends still farther, how-

ever. Just as, for Descartes, the experience of God as, in effect, a violator of his mind, as one who "breaks" his *cogito,*
goes with a profound sense of *obligation,* and with an experience of glory, so, for Levinas, the experience of the Other
as, in effect, a violator of his mind, as one who breaks his
phenomenology, goes with what I called the "fundamental obligation" to make oneself available to the Other, and
with the experience of what Levinas calls "the Glory of
the Infinite."[24] Indeed, it is a part of Levinas's strategy to
regularly transfer predicates to the Other that traditional
theology ascribes to God (hence Levinas's talk of my "infinite responsibility" to the Other, of the impossibility of
really seeing the face of the Other, of the "height" of the
Other, etc.).

WHAT TO MAKE OF THIS

It is important to keep in mind that Levinas does not intend to replace traditional metaphysics and epistemology
with a *different,* nontraditional, metaphysics and epistemology. Merely replacing the phenomenalism of Carnap
or the phenomenology of Husserl with the kind of realism
currently favored by many analytic philosophers would not
satisfy Levinas at all. Such a metaphysics does just as much
violence to the agent point of view as does the phenomenalism of Carnap or the transcendental phenomenology
of Husserl. In the metaphysical realist picture, as Thomas
Nagel has stressed (but without abandoning that picture
himself), the agent point of view disappears in favor of "the
view from nowhere."

What Levinas wants to remind us of is precisely the
underivability of what I called the fundamental obligation
from any metaphysical or epistemological picture. Each
of Levinas's principle tropes—*infinite responsibility, face versus trace, height*—connects with the two fundamental ideas

that *ethics is based on obligation to the other, not on any empirical or metaphysical "sameness" between myself and the other* and that this fundamental obligation is *asymmetrical.*

(i) *Infinite Responsibility:* I have already explained what I think Levinas means by talk of "infinity" in this connection. But what of "responsibility"?

An ancient Jewish principle holds that *kol yisrael 'arevim zeh lazeh*—every Israelite is responsible for every other. The corresponding Levinasian claim is that every human being is responsible for every other. Levinas puts it in just these terms: in a discussion of a passage in the Talmud (*Sotah* 37), which talks about the various occasions upon which Israel covenanted with God, Levinas writes:[25]

> A moment ago, we saw a part played [in a remark by Rabbi Mesharsheya] by something resembling the recognition of the Other, the love of the Other. To such an extent that I offer myself as a guarantee of the other, of his adherence and fidelity to the Law. His concern is my concern. But is not my concern also his? Isn't he responsible for me? And if he is, can I answer for his responsibility for me? *kol yisrael 'arevim zeh lazeh,* All Israel is responsible one for the other, which means, all those who cleave to the divine law, all men worthy of the name, are responsible for each other.

"All men worthy of the name are responsible for each other." But Levinas in the next sentences immediately stresses the theme of asymmetry:

> I always have, myself, one responsibility more than anyone else, since I am responsible, in addition, for his responsibility. And if he is responsible for my responsibility, I remain responsible for the responsibility he has for my responsibility. *Ein ladavar sof,* 'it will never end'. In the society of the Torah, this process is repeated to infinity; beyond any responsibility attributed to everyone and for everyone, there is always the additional fact that I am responsible for that responsibility. It is

an ideal, but one which is inseparable for the humanity of human beings. . . .

(ii) *Face versus Trace:* Levinas speaks of the "nonphenomenality of the face,"[26] and he goes on to say:

> In the obsession with this nudity and this poverty, this withdrawal or this dying, where synthesis and contemporaneousness are refused, proximity, as though it were an abyss, interrupts being's unrendable essence.[27] A face approached, a contact with a skin—a face weighed down with a skin, and a skin in which, even in obscenity, the altered face breathes—are already absent from themselves. . . .

And on the very next page,[28]

> Phenomenology defects into a face, even if, in the course of this ever ambiguous defecting of appearing, the obsession itself shows itself in the said.[29] The appearing is broken by the young epiphany, the still essential beauty of a face. But this use is already past in this youth; the skin is with wrinkles, a trace of itself, the ambiguous form of a supreme presence attending to its appearing, breaking through its plastic form with youth, but already a failing of all presence, less than a phenomenon, already a poverty that hides its wretchedness and orders me.

Here part of the idea is that even when I stare at your physical face, at your skin itself, I do not "see you face to face" in the biblical sense, do not and cannot encounter the you that "hides its wretchedness and orders me." I see in this the Levinasian trope of transferring attributes of God to the Other.[30] Just as we never see God, but at best traces of God's presence in the world, so we never see the "face" of the Other, but only its "trace." But the emphasis on "wretchedness and suffering" isn't connected *only* with awareness that the other is mortal, although it *is* textually connected with that.[31] It is also connected with Levinas's emphasis on the neediness of others and the corresponding obligation on the "me" who always has "one responsibility more than anyone else" to sacrifice for others, to the point of substituting for them, to the point of martyrdom—a demand I shall comment on at the end of this chapter. In Levinas's image of man, the *vulnerability* of the other is what is stressed, in contrast to what Levinas sees as the Enlightenment's radiant image of the human essence.

(iii) *Height:* Here is Levinas's own explanation of this trope, in one of the conversations with Philippe Nemo:

> Ph.N.: In the face of the Other you say there is an "elevation," a "height." The Other is higher than I am. What do you mean by that?
>
> E.L. The first word of the face is the "Thou shalt not Kill." It is an order. [Again the Other is given a God-like attribute!— HP] There is a commandment in the appearance of the face, as if a master spoke to me. However, at the same time, the face of the Other is destitute; it is the poor for whom I can do all and to whom I owe all. And me, whoever I may be, but as a "first person," I am he who finds the resources to respond to the call.
>
> Ph.N. One is tempted to say to you: yes, in certain cases. But in other cases, to the contrary, the encounter with the Other occurs in the mode of violence, hate and disdain.
>
> E.L. To be sure. But I think that whatever the motivation which explains this inversion, the analysis of the face such as I have just made, with the mastery of the Other and his poverty, with my submission and my wealth, is primary. It is the presupposed in all human relationships. If it were not that, we would not even say, before an open door, "after you, sir!" It is an original "After you, sir!" that I have tried to describe.[32]

THE VALUE OF JUDAISM (FOR GENTILES)

The thesis I am defending is that in understanding the thought of this profoundly original thinker, it is essential to understand two facts: (1) that Levinas is drawing on Jewish sources and themes, and (2) (paradoxically, since Levinas is an *Orthodox* Jew), Levinas is *universalizing* Judaism.

It is necessary, however, to keep in mind that Levinas's Judaism exhibits a "Lithuanian" distrust of the charismatic.[33] If Christianity valorizes the moment when an individual feels the charismatic presence of the Savior entering into his/her life, Judaism, as Levinas presents it, distrusts the charismatic. Thus he writes in "A Religion for Adults":

> But all [Judaism's] efforts—from the Bible to the closure of the Talmud in the sixth century and throughout most of its commentators from the great era of rabbinical science—consists in its understanding the saintliness of God in a sense that stands in sharp contrast to the numinous meaning of this term . . . Judaism remains foreign to any offensive return of these forms of human elevation. It denounces them as the essence of idolatry.
>
> The numinous or the Sacred envelops and transports man beyond his powers and wishes, but a true liberty takes offense at this uncontrollable surplus . . . This somehow sacramental power of the Divine seems to Judaism to offend human freedom and to be contrary to the education of man, which remains *action on a free being.* Not that liberty is an end in itself, but it does remain the condition for any value man may attain. The Sacred that envelops and transports me is a form of violence.[34]

And in "For a Jewish Humanism," Levinas writes, "The *no* with which the Jews, so dangerously over the centuries, replied to the calls of the Church does not express an absurd stubbornness, but the conviction that important human truths in the Old Testament were being lost in the theology of the New."[35]

What are these "important human truths" that Levinas is universalizing? Obviously, his notion of "Judaism" is both selective and idiosyncratic.[36] But it is not without a basis. Rabbinic Judaism was utterly transformed after the fall of the Temple. The transformation involved subjecting all religious texts, including the Jewish Bible itself, to a literally unending process of interpretation (David Hartman has recently described the Jewish people as a "community of interpretation.").[37] The founding generation of Rabbinic Judaism, the generation that saw the destruction of Jerusalem and began the construction of a new, non-Temple-based mode of worship at Jabne, included such figures as Rabbi Johanan ben Zakkai, Rabbi Gamaliel, Rabbi Joshua ben Hananiah, and the immensely learned Rabbi Eliezer ben Hyrcanus. A story in the Talmud (Baba Metzia 59a–b) relates that in a dispute with some of the other members of the group at Jabne, Eliezer ben Hyrcanus called for a series of miracles (which then occurred) including a "heavenly voice" (*bat kol*) to prove that he was right and *lost the debate in spite of the heavenly voice and the miracles.* "We pay no heed to a heavenly voice," the rabbis told God, "for you have already written in the Torah at Mount Sinai, 'to incline after a multitude'."[38] The Talmud goes on to give us God's reaction. Rabbi Nathan, it relates, "happening upon" the prophet Elijah, asked what God had done at that hour. "He smiled," Elijah said, "and said: My children have vanquished me, my children have vanquished me!"

While some of the commentators in the Talmud itself assert that the miracles were only dreamt and did not actually occur, there is no question that at this crucial meeting at Jabne Judaism took a turn away from what Levinas calls the "numinous." Human autonomy was henceforth to have a voice in determining what the Divine Commandment *means*.[39] It is true that in the Pentateuch Moses is described as having a numinous experience at Sinai, but that experience is not taken as a model for the religious experience of the traditional Jew. Rather, the position of the traditional Jew is one of feeling a profound experience of being Commanded by a God of whom she or he has *not* had a numinous experience. The "trace" of God's presence is the tradition that testifies to the Commandment and the interpretative community that continues to work out what it means.

Levinas modifies this picture, for at least two reasons. First of all, his intended audience, as I have stressed, is not just Jews but humanity as a whole. And, secondly, even if he universalizes certain Jewish themes, he does not attempt to *convert* the gentiles to Judaism. He is not trying to emulate St. Paul. The detailed *mitzvot* ("commandments") are not what he wants his "universal" audience to learn about or obey (which is what they would have to do, among other things, to convert to Judaism), but rather the fundamental commandment that Rabbi Hillel the Elder gave in two famous forms: "Love mankind"[40] and "What is hateful to you do not do to your fellow man; this is the whole Torah, the rest is mere commentary."[41]

Thus the "important human truths in the Old Testament," as interpreted by Levinas, include the following: (1) that every human being should experience him/herself as *commanded* to be available to the neediness, the suffering, the vulnerability of the other person. This is to be as binding upon one's very soul as the commandments to love God and to love your neighbor as yourself are in the eyes of someone who lives up to the normative Jewish ideal of piety; indeed, like Hillel, Levinas thinks "the rest is mere commentary." (2) One can—indeed, one must— *know* that this is commanded of one without a philosophical account of how this is possible. (What makes this strain in Levinas's thought "Jewish" is the remarkable fact that the Talmud, although produced in a Hellenistic environment in which scholars claimed that every educated person was somewhat acquainted with Platonic and post-Platonic philosophy, fails to refer to that philosophy *in any way.* Only a handful of Jewish figures—Philo of Alexandria, for example—attempted to synthesize Greek philosophy and Jewish religion, and not until the tenth, eleventh, and twelfth centuries (with such figures as Saadia Gaon, Bahya ibn Paquda, and Abraham ibn Ezra, as well as, of course Maimonides) did the attempt have any significant influence (and even then, Maimonides' codification of Jewish Law was more influential than his philosophy). (3) My knowledge that "I myself" have received a divine command not only lacks a metaphysical basis, but it is also not based on anything like a personal epiphany. I have only a "trace" of the Commander, never an epiphany.

The Value of Judaism (for Jews)

If Levinas is trying to universalize fundamental Jewish values when he speaks to the gentile world, it is also true that, to a certain extent, he *resists* universalism when speaking to the Jewish world—especially to Jews who participate in modern culture and who, like himself, value many of the achievements of that culture. Thus in a moving essay titled "Judaism and the Present," Levinas writes, "In the wake of the Liberation, Jews[42] are grappling with the Angel of Reason who often solicited them and who for two centuries now has refused to let go. Despite the experience of Hitler and the failure of assimilation, *the great vocation in life resounds like the call of a universal and homogenous society.*"[43]

Levinas goes on to urge resistance to this call of the Angel of Reason. However, Levinas's notion of resisting "a universal and homogenous society" does not require combating liberalizing movements within Judaism such as Reform Judaism. In the next sentences, in fact, Levinas writes, "We do not have to decide here if the nature of modern life is compatible with respect for the Sabbath and rituals concerning food or if we should lighten the yoke of the Law. These important questions are put to men who have already chosen Judaism. They chose between orthodoxy and reform depending on their ideas of rigor, courage and duty. Some are not necessarily hypocrites, others do not always take the easy way out. *But it is really a domestic quarrel*" [emphasis added—HP].

Nor does resistance to the Angel of Reason require that one believe in the *literal* truth of the doctrine that the Pentateuch—and, in the traditional Jewish account, the "oral Torah," the Talmud, as well—were given to Moses by God on Mount Sinai). On the next page and its sequel Levinas writes:

> . . . Judaism had been threatened before. Cosmology and scientific history in their time had compromised the Bible's wisdom, while philology had questioned the special character of the Bible itself, dissolved in a sea of texts, pitching and rolling through its infinite undulations. Apologetics chose to reply to these attacks by discussing the arguments put forward. But believers have all resisted them by interiorizing certain religious truths. Why worry about science's refutations of Biblical cosmology, when the Bible contains not cosmology but images necessary to an unshakable inner certainty, figures that speak to the religious soul that dwells in the absolute? Why worry about philology and history challenging the supposed date and origin of the sacred texts, if these texts are intrinsically rich in value? The sacred sparks of individual revelations have produced the light needed, even if they were thrown up at different points in history. The miracle of their convergence is no less marvelous than the miracle of a unique source.[44]

At this point, Levinas enters into an intricate dialectic.[45] "The eternity of Israel is not the privilege of a nation that is proud or carried away by illusions," he tells us, but "it has a function in the economy of being. It is indispensable to the work of reason itself." Justice, he argues, "needs a stable base," and this stable base cannot be a mere abstraction, not even abstract reason, but can only be "an interiority, a person." "A person is indispensable to justice prior to being indispensable to himself." He briefly digresses to criticize Sartre, pointing out that those who stress commitment in Sartre's work forget that Sartre's main concern was to guarantee disengagement (*degagément*) in the midst of engagement. But "dumping ballast in the face of the problems posed by existence, in order to gain even greater height over reality, leads ultimately to the impossibility of sacrifice, that is to say the annihilation of self," Levinas argues.

What is Judaism's alternative to this *degagément,* to the attempt to stand above reality or to bring justice down to reality from some abstract level? Judaism affirms "the fidelity to a law, a moral standard." But "[t]his is not the return to the status of a thing, for such fidelity breaks the facile enchantment of cause and effect and allows it to be judged."[46] And in a passage strikingly reminiscent of Rosenzweig's claim in *The Star of Redemption* that Judaism stands completely outside the Hegelian dialectic of "world historic" religions and civilizations, Levinas writes as follows:[47]

> Judaism is a non-coincidence with its time, within coincidence: in the radical sense of the term, it is an *anachronism,* the simultaneous presence of a youth that is attentive to reality and impatient to change it, and an old age that has seen it all and is returning to the origin of things.[48] The desire to conform to one's time is not the supreme imperative for a human, but is

already a characteristic expression of modernism itself; it involves renouncing interiority and truth, resigning oneself to death, and, in base souls, being satisfied with *jouissance*. Monotheism and its moral revelation constitute the concrete fulfillment, beyond all mythology, of the primordial anachronism of the human.

It is noteworthy that this defense of Jewish particularism is itself couched in universalistic language. That ethics cannot be founded on reason but must be founded on the aspiration to be "face-to-face with the other" (even if all we actually see is the "trace" of one another's faces), on the willingness to sacrifice for the other, to substitute ourselves for the other's suffering, and that this one Commandment is analogous to a fissure in being, and that the aspiration of Western thought to include everything in its "View from Nowhere" (to revert to Nagel's phrase) must be resisted on *moral* grounds, are things that, if true, are true for *everyone*. Yet the essay from which I have been quoting is an appeal to young Jews not to "turn their backs on Judaism because, like a waking dream, it does not offer them sufficient enlightenment concerning contemporary problems." They forget, Levinas tells them, "that revelation offers clarification but not a formula; they forget that commitment alone—commitment at any price, headlong commitment that burns its bridges behind it . . . is no less inhuman than the disengagement dictated by the desire to be comfortable which ossifies a society that has transformed the difficult task of Judaism into a mere confession, an accessory of bourgeois comfort."[49]

Is Levinas simply reducing what he calls "Judaism" to his own unique brand of ethical monotheism?

If asked what *really* characterizes Orthodox Judaism (and Levinas was an Orthodox Jew, even if a rather heterodox one), I suppose most Jews would reply "study and *mitzvot*." Where do these enter, if they do, into what Levinas is here calling "Judaism"?—But I need to explain "study and *mitzvot.*"

Mitzvah (plural *mitzvot*) is translated "commandment," but the translation is doubly misleading (although literally correct!). It is misleading, first, because "commandment" cannot help evoking "the Ten Commandments," and the Ten Commandments are referred to in the Jewish Bible as the ten *d'varim,* the ten sayings, not the ten *mitzvot.* It is misleading, secondly, because while every religion has "commandments," not every religion has *mitzvot.* What is characteristic of *mitzvot* is that they form a *system,* a system whose function is to sanctify every possible portion of life, including the parts described as "profane." "Keeping *mitzvot*" is an entire way of life, a way that is supposed to glorify God and exemplify justice.

The image of the fundamental obligation as analogous to a commandment from God (a commandment from the Infinite) is central to Levinas's whole way of thinking. But Levinas certainly does not say everyone should keep *mitzvot,* for example, by keeping the Jewish Sabbath or observing the Jewish dietary laws. Indeed, he is surprisingly tolerant of Jews who think that "modern life" requires that "we should lighten the yoke of the Law" (the determination of just what *mitzvot* an observant Jew is required to keep), perhaps because he sees them as Jews who left traditional devotional life in order to respond to calls for justice.

Study is one of the *mitzvot,* but it is also described as "equal to all" the *mitzvot* and good deeds put together, because it leads to them.[50] What is most distinctive about traditional Jewish religiosity is the emphasis placed on study, and especially study of the Talmud (after the Bible itself, the founding text, or rather texts, of Judaism), and upon interpretation of the Jewish law.

Whereas I have not been able to find in Levinas any

sustained discussion of *mitzvot*, in his emphasis on study of the Jewish texts he is at one with the tradition. Levinas (although not, by scholarly standards, a distinguished Talmudist) never tired of lecturing on and interpreting passages in the Talmud, often reading his own philosophy into these passages, but nonetheless communicating the joy of Talmud study. In "Judaism and the Present," after stressing the "anachronistic" character of Judaism, and explaining how this differs from "this false eternity" (the eternity of "dead civilizations such as Greece or Rome"),[51] Levinas goes on to say,

> But this essential content, which history cannot touch, cannot be learned like a catechism or resumed like a credo. Nor is it restricted to the negative and formal statement of the categorical imperative. It cannot be replaced by Kantianism, nor, to an even lesser degree, can it be obtained from some particular privilege or racial miracle. It is acquired through a way of living that is a ritual and a heart-felt generosity, wherein a human fraternity and an attention to the present are reconciled with an eternal distance in relation to the contemporary world. It is an asceticism, like the training of a fighter. It is acquired and held, finally, in the particular type of intellectual life known as study of the Torah, that permanent revision and updating of the content of Revelation, where every situation within the human adventure can be judged. And it is here precisely that the Revelation is to be found: the die is not cast, the prophets or wise men of the Talmud knew nothing about antibiotics or nuclear energy; but the categories needed to understand these novelties are already available to monotheism. It is the eternal anteriority of wisdom with respect to science and history. Without it, success would equal reason and reason would just be the necessity of living in one's own time.[52]

Here, then, is where the universalization of Judaism stops, and the resistance to universalism begins. True, when Levinas is addressing gentiles (or the so-called "general public"), he also opposes the universalization of abstract reason, and also teaches that "interiority, a person" is where we should look to find a stable foundation for justice and ethics. But he never attempts to tell gentiles what *their* equivalent to the "ritual and the heart-felt generosity" of traditional Judaism, their equivalent to "the particular type of intellectual life known as study of the Torah," might be.

GOD IS WITHOUT CONTENT APART FROM THE RELATION TO THE OTHER

For Levinas, God, or "the Infinite," is unthematizable.[53] That does not mean the notion is contentless; for there is the possibility (which Buber is accused of overlooking) that "transcendence without any dogmatic content can receive a content from the dimension of height,"[54] that is, from my experiencing "the glory of the Infinite" *through* the "height of the other."

Here is a description of this possibility (in *Otherwise than Being*):

> The ego stripped by the trauma of persecution of its scornful and imperialist subjectivity, is reduced to the "here I am" [*hineni!*—HP] as a witness of the Infinite, but a witness that does not thematize what it bears witness of, and whose truth is not the truth of representation, is not evidence.[55] There is witness, a unique structure, an exception to the rule of being,[56] irreducible to representation, only of the Infinite. The infinite does not appear to him that bears witness to it. It is by the voice of the witness that the glory of the Infinite is glorified.[57]

Yet, in spite of the religious feeling we sense here, the Infinite has no content beyond its ethical content. Levinas is emphatic about this. For example, in one of his discussions with Philippe Nemo, Levinas himself raises the question of the content of the word *God* in his writing, and answers:

> You are thinking: what becomes of the Infinity that the title *Totality and Infinity* announced? To my mind the Infinite comes in the signifyingness of the face. The face *signifies* the Infinite. It never appears a theme, but in this ethical signifyingness itself; that is the fact that the more I am just the more I am responsible; one is never quits with regard to the Other.[58]

APPRECIATION AND SOME OBJECTIONS

How is one to identify Levinas's unique contribution to twentieth-century thought? To say, as the dust jacket of *The Levinas Reader* does, that he provided "inspiration for Derrida, Lyotard, Blanchot and Irigaray" is not, for all of us, an unmixed compliment!

I shall begin with a remark by Harry Frankfurt (in conversation) to the effect that there is a certain similarity between Levinas's thought and the thought of the ethical intuitionists. What I want to do is identify both the element of truth in the comparison and the limits of any such comparison.

Like the intuitionists, Levinas does not appeal to abstract arguments to ground ethics. What I called "the fundamental obligation to say *hineni* to the other" is something one is expected to feel, not arrive at by abstract reason. But there is an important difference, especially from Moore: perception of my obligation to the other in all its dimensions is grounded in my relation to the other as a *person*. For Moore, the ethical intuition is almost Platonic: I perceive a "non-natural quality." For other intuitionists it is not Moorean "goodness" that I am supposed to intuit but *obligation as such*. But for Levinas if there is anything I "intuit" it is *the presence of the other person*.

In this respect it might appear that Levinas is closer to Hume than to the intuitionists. For Hume too, after all, ethics is grounded on our reactions to people, not to Platonic universals or other "non-natural" entities. But, as we have already seen, there is an important difference: for Hume, it is the perception of the *sameness* of the other person, my *sympathy* for the other person, that is the sine qua non. But, Levinas tells us, that isn't good enough. If you only feel obligated to those with whom you sympathize, or if you only sympathize with those whom you can see as "like me," then you are not ethical at all (a point already made by Kant). Indeed, Levinas would say, you are still trapped within your own ego—that is, your "ethics" is, at bottom, narcissism.

At the same time, Levinas is very far from Kant. For Kant, ethics is fundamentally a matter of *principles* and of *reason;* the experience of the "dignity" of accepting a principle and acting on a principle from Reason alone is the ethical experience par excellence. For Levinas—and I agree with him here—the indispensable experience is the experience of responding to another person, where neither the other person nor my response are seen at that crucial moment as instances of universals. The other is not an instance of any abstraction, not even "humanity"; she is who she is. And my response is not an instance of any abstract rule, not even the Categorical Imperative. It is simply a matter of doing what I am "called on" to do, then and there.

What is original (and I think important and powerful) here is the idea that ethics can—and must—be based on a relation to people, but a relation that is totally free of narcissism, with the further emphasis that to be free of narcissism one must respect the "alterity" of the other, the other's manifold difference. My awareness of my ethical obligation must not depend on any "gesture" of claiming (literally or figuratively) to "comprehend" the other. I do not know any other ethical philosopher who has so powerfully combined the idea that ethics is based on the perception of *persons*, not of abstractions, with the idea that the ethical perception must fully respect alterity.

The third central Levinasian idea—so central that it is hard to find any place where Levinas responds to an interlocutor without mentioning it—is the *asymmetry* of the ethical relation. The primordial attitude (I shall call it an "attitude" even if Levinas would not) that is the Levinasian sine qua non for entering the ethical life—which is to say, entering *human* life, in any sense that is "worthy of the name"—involves recognizing that one is *obligated* to make oneself available to the neediness of the other *without* simultaneously regarding the other as so obligated. Levinas is the very opposite of a "contractarian" in this respect.

When I say that, for Levinas, the ethical life is the only life that can, in a normative sense, be called "human," I do not merely mean to be "paying a compliment" to the ethical life (as Richard Rorty might put it). In Levinas's phenomenology, not to have entered the ethical life, not to have been "obsessed" by "the height of the other," is to be trapped within one's own ego. Without ethics one cannot even enter into the *world*, in this picture.

All of this I find powerful and compelling. But I shall conclude with some criticisms of certain aspects of Levinas's philosophy that I find problematic.

In another of the discussions with Philippe Nemo, Levinas says:[59]

> I have previously said elsewhere—I do not like mentioning it for it should be completed by other considerations—that I am responsible for the persecutions that I undergo. But only me! My 'close relations' or 'my people' are already the others and, for them, I demand justice.

[Philipe Nemo: You go that far!]

[Levinas:] Since I am responsible even for the Other's responsibility. These are extreme formulas which must not be detached from their context. In the concrete, many other considerations intervene and require justice even for me. Practically, the laws set certain consequences out of the way. But justice only has meaning if it retains the spirit of dis-interestedness which animates the idea of responsibility for the other man. In principle the I does not pull itself out of its 'first person'; it supports the world. Constituting itself in the very movement wherein being responsible for the other devolves upon it, subjectivity goes to the point of substitution for the Other. It assumes the condition—or the uncondition—of hostage. Subjectivity as such is inherently hostage; it answers to the point of expiation for others.

One can appear scandalized by this utopian and, for an I, inhuman conception. But the humanity of the human—the true life—is absent.[60]

I must admit to being one of those who are "scandalized by this utopian . . . inhuman conception." That is not what I want to focus on in this quotation, but let me say that one can accept all of the Levinasian insights that I find compelling without agreeing that, in the absence of the conditions that "intervene in the concrete," I am responsible to the point of responsibility for my own persecution (in other contexts: to the point of offering myself as a substitute for the other—think of a concentration camp!—to the point of martyrdom). It is true that someone who would not give his life for anyone else, for his family or his friends or even his whole people, has not reached the level of "the human—the true life." This is something it does not take Levinas to say; the Utilitarians know this full well. It is also true that someone who would give his life for an ideology or an abstraction but not for another person has, in a different way, missed "the human—the true life." But, the "asymmetry" of the ethical relation need not be carried as far as Levinas carries it. And—incorrigible Aristotelian that I am—I would not carry it that far. It is, I think, because Levinas thinks of ethics as the *whole* of "the true life" that he does so. But to be *only* ethical, even if one be ethical to the point of martyrdom, is to live a *one-sided* life.

But I said that that is not what I wanted to focus on in this quotation. What I want to focus on are a few words that may seem almost incidental: "In the concrete, many other considerations intervene and require justice even for me."

My quarrel is not with the idea that justice is required by the need to reconcile conflicting ethical demands. (The idea that one can explain the need for justice in purely reductionist terms seems to me mistaken.) What troubles me is the fact that this dialectic of an *extreme* statement followed by a vague statement to the effect that "in the concrete, many other considerations intervene and require justice even for me" occurs more than once in Levinas writing. For example, in *Otherwise than Being*, "This condition or unconditionality of being a hostage will then at least be an essential modality of freedom, the first, and not an empirical accident of the freedom, proud in itself, of the ego."—*Immediately* followed by: "To be sure—but this is another theme—my responsibility for all can and has to manifest itself also in limiting itself. The ego can, in the name of this unlimited responsibility, be called on to concern itself also with itself. The fact that the other, my neighbor, is also a third party with respect to another, who is also a neighbor, is the birth of thought, consciousness, justice and philosophy." [61]

Here Levinas seems to simultaneously restate his "utopian," his "unlimited" vision of human responsibility and reassure us that in practice it is not so utopian after all.

I agree that one should not demand unlimited responsibility in practice; but not only because I am a neighbor of my neighbor.

I mentioned Aristotle. It is Aristotle who taught us that to love others one must be able to love oneself. The thought seems utterly alien to Levinas, for whom, it seems, I can at best see myself as one loved by those whom I love.[62] But I think Aristotle was right. I also described Levinas's ethics cum phenomenology as "one-sided." It is because it is one-sided that, I think, Levinas relation to Buber is fundamentally a *competitive* one. Rather than see Buber as someone who identified a *different* "I-Thou" relation than Levinas's, someone who identified a different sine qua non of the "true life," Levinas must see Buber as someone who (had insights to be sure, but) *got it wrong.* But the ethical life has more than one sine qua non.

Isaiah Berlin famously divided thinkers into "hedgehogs" (who know "one big thing") and foxes (who know "many small things"). But, *pace* Berlin, it isn't just a choice between hedgehogs and foxes. Where the ethical life is concerned, there are quite a few "big things" to be known. We need many hedgehogs. And certainly one of the "hedgehogs" we need to listen to is Emmanuel Levinas.

Afterword

In the preceding chapters, I have only in passing indicated my own religious attitudes because, as I explained in the introduction, my concern in writing this book was to help a reader who is willing to struggle with these difficult authors to understand their difficult and spiritually deep writings, and not to present those attitudes. Another reason is that I do not for one moment delude myself into thinking that my own reflections, however important they may be to me, are deep religious philosophy in the way that the writings I have been discussing are profound. But the reader who has been trusting and patient enough to accept me as a guide this far certainly deserves at least a brief answer to the question, "but where do *you* stand?"

I did say in the introduction that in a conversation I recently had with an old friend, I described my current religious standpoint as "somewhere between John Dewey in *A Common Faith* and Martin Buber."

Let me now explain what I meant by that.

In *A Common Faith*, Dewey recognizes that our religious experiences and the conduct that they inspire often have great value. That they can also have negative aspects is something he is well aware of, from, for example, his struggle with the tortured feelings of guilt that he suffered in his youth (and that his biographers ascribe to the extreme version of Calvinism to which his mother subscribed), and from his disappointment at the fact that in his lifetime organized religions so often sided with the powers that be at times of social protest. Indeed, *organized* religion is not something Dewey ever came to favor. But in his short book, Dewey views God as a human projection that embodies our highest ideals.

By this, I understand Dewey to be saying that the kind of reality God has is the reality of an ideal. Some people, we know, feel that this kind of reality is merely subjective. But Dewey did not believe that ideas and values are "subjective" in the sense of being outside the spheres of rational argument and objective validity. Our values and ideals are indeed subjective in the sense of being the values of *subjects*, of human individuals and communities. But which values and ideals enable us to grow and flourish is not a mere matter of "subjective opinion"; it is something one can be right or wrong about.

Perhaps some will also say that even if ideals and values can be objectively right, in Dewey's pragmatist sense, in which objective rightness is reappraisable and revisable, still the reality of an ideal is something pale, something "intellectual." But it takes only a moment's thought to realize that that is not the case, at least not with a *living* ideal. Think how often such ideals as equality and justice have called forth deeds of great courage and dedication. If these ideals had not at times been overwhelmingly "real" to some individuals, notwithstanding the circumstance that they are woefully far from being *realized*, this would be a far more intolerable world than it is.

Like Dewey, I do not believe in an afterlife, or in God as a supernatural helper who intervenes in the course of history or in the course of our lives to rescue us from disasters. I don't believe in "miracles" in *that* sense. But spirituality—in my case, that means praying, meditating, putting myself in touch with the ideals, rituals, ancient texts, that the Jewish people have passed down for more than two millennia, and undergoing the experiences that go with all of these—is miraculous and natural at the same time, just as the contact with another in what Buber calls the "I-You" relation is miraculous and natural, and the contact with natural beauty or with art can be miraculous and natural.

But God is not an ideal of the same kind as Equality or Justice. The traditional believer—and this is something I share with the traditional believer, even if I don't share his or her belief in an afterlife, or in the supernatural—visualizes God as a supremely wise, kind, just person. Although many intellectuals are afraid of this sort of "anthropomorphism" because they are afraid (as Maimonides was already afraid) that it will be taken literally, I feel that it need not be "taken literally," but is still far more valuable than any metaphysical concept of an impersonal God, let alone a God who is "totally other." Thus I understand, in my own way to be sure, what Buber is talking about when he speaks of an "I-You" relation to God. (And, if I am wrong about the "nature" of God, that is, in the end, not so important if Buber is right, for thinking about "the nature of God" is third-person thinking, and that is just what Buber wants us to give up.)

In the preceding chapters, I have tried to bring out

what I find most attractive in the thinking of each of the great Jewish thinkers we have studied, because each of them has something to say to me. Now I want to say something about what they have in common, other than the mere fact of having lived in the twentieth century. For I do see them a having had much in common, notwithstanding differences in what would traditionally be called their "metaphysics."

First, however, let us acknowledge those differences, for they are substantial:

(1) For Rosenzweig, at least one "ontological" thesis is insistently repeated: the utter *distinctness* of God, Man, and World. The distinctness of God from the other two means, in particular, that all theologies that make God in any way a human construct are "atheistic theologies."[1] (I must admit that in Rosenzweig's eyes I would have counted as an "atheist theologian.") What is surprising is that Rosenzweig regards Man and World as just as distinct as Man and God. Traditional philosophy and theology (not to mention common sense) regard man as *part* of the world. To be sure, Man has gifts that other animals do not have—in traditional religions, Man is supposed to have an immortal soul—but he is not distinct from the world altogether (in traditional thinking, either Jewish or Christian), in the way he seems to be in Part One of the *Star*. Moreover, the immortality that concerns Rosenzweig seems not to be personal immortality but the immortality of the Jewish people. It may be that insisting on the total distinctness of Man and World is Rosenzweig's way of rejecting the idealist view that the World is a human construct, just as insisting on the total distinctness of God and World is his way of rejecting the idea that he sees in early Buber, that God is a human construct.

(2) Martin Buber, as we saw in chapter 3, tells us not

to theorize about God in the third person, but to *address* God. I feel a deep sympathy with this aspect of Buber's thought. For now, let me just observe that the question of the "nonidentity" of God, Man, and World that exercises Rosenzweig does not arise in that form for Buber. When I think of "World" as a collection of *things,* then, of course, I relate to it as a *mere* (untransfigured) "It-world," and this is totally different from any "I-Thou" relation that I may enter into with God or with other persons. In that sense, God is totally different from the world and other persons are totally different from the world. But the world is not only the subject of "I-It" relations in *I and Thou:* there are also "I-Thou" relations that we enter into at moments with many things in the world, including parts of nature (trees, Buber's cat) and particular works of art. So the unique-ness of God is not an absolute gulf here. And if one is for-tunate enough to experience an "I-Thou" relation to God, then, Buber tells us, one will find all one's other (positive) I-Thou relations "taken up" in it; in that respect God is dif-ferent from any human person. But again there is no ques-tion of an ontological gulf here, because Buber is not doing ontology: he is warning us away from ontological specu-lation as a trap that can only lead away from an authentic religious encounter.

(3) For Levinas, all we know of God is what he asks of us: total willingness to help the other. But that does not mean that Levinas's philosophy consists merely of an eth-ics. This becomes clear in two ways. First, as we described in chapter 4, according to Levinas my encounter with the other is an encounter with a *fissure,* an encounter with a being who breaks my categories. Secondly, although I do not encounter God in anything like Buber's "I-Thou" rela-tion, I do encounter "the glory of the infinite" when I as-sume the (profoundly asymmetric) relation to the other

that Levinas believes is demanded of me. In both of these aspects of Levinas's philosophy, we have the only version of the *supernatural*—or, better, the superontological—that Levinas will entertain as a philosopher: the superontological is what is outside of the possibility of human thought at all, because it is outside the categories within which we have to think. Not that I cannot think of the other person at all—obviously I can—but I both realize and cannot succeed in grasping the "alterity," the fundamental *otherness* of the other. Similarly, I can think that I ought to help another person, and I may believe (if I am religious) that this is what God wants of me, but I both realize and cannot succeed in grasping the fact that this is a *divinely* commanded action. What violates my categories can only be apprehended fleetingly, mystically—as the "trace" of the other's face, as the "glory" of the Infinite. Ethics is first philosophy because "philosophy" in the sense of ontology isn't up to the job of describing either the Infinite or the other in all the other's alterity. And philosophy isn't up to the job because human intellection isn't up to the job.

Comparing Levinas with Rosenzweig in this respect, we may say that even Rosenzweig's repeated assertions of the "nonidentity" of Man, God, and World would be impossible for Levinas: the very title of one of Levinas's late books, *Beyond Essence or Otherwise than Being*, emphasizes that notions such as "identity" and "nonidentity" simply make no sense in connection with God. And Levinas criticizes Buber's notion of an "I-Thou" relation as well; the "I-Thou" relation Levinas wants us to have with the other is an *asymmetrical* one.[2]

In one way of looking at them, these differences are enormous. A metaphysics that insists on the thesis of the absolute nonidentity of Man, God, and World; a religious philosophy that denies the very possibility of theorizing about God as if he were a "third person"; and a religious philosophy that insists that God and the other are both "otherwise than being"—in an academic philosopher's way of thinking, these are totally different. But the academic philosopher's way of thinking misses the point.

To see that the differences between these philosophers are not of crucial importance, let us recall what Rosenzweig told us about the *Star* in the essay titled "The New Thinking."[3] I have already quoted from this essay in chapter 2. Let us look again at two of those quotations. First,

> What is said here [in Part I of the *Star*] is nothing other than a *reductio ad absurdum* and, at the same time, a rescue of the old philosophy. (114–115)

—and again:

> Experience, no matter how deeply it may penetrate, discovers only the human in man, only worldliness in the world, only divinity in God. And only in God divinity, only in the world worldliness, and only in man the human. *Finis Philosophiae?*[4] If it were, then so much the worse for philosophy! But I do not believe that it turns out so badly. Rather, at this point where philosophy would certainly be at an end with its thinking, experiential philosophy can begin. In any case, that is the point of my first volume [i.e., of Part I of the *Star*]. (116–117)

Here we see that what I called "a metaphysics that insists on the thesis of the absolute nonidentity of Man, God, and World" belongs to the less important part of the philosophy of the *Star*, to the part that brings us to the point of seeing that what we need is "experiential philosophy." And "experiential philosophy" is another term for "the new thinking," that is, for the idea that the philosophical activity that is most important is the activity that deals with the lived problems of human interlocutors, and that proceeds by genuine dialogue and not by lecturing.

In the end, the "new thinking" is a philosophy that is supposed to take place within "I-You" encounters. And similarly, Levinas's idea of God as breaking all of our categories is a warning against attempts to "account" for God within a phenomenology of either a Husserlian or a Heideggerian kind.

It is worthwhile, I believe, to contrast the sense in which any one of these three thinkers is a "negative theologian" with the sense in which Maimonides was a negative theologian. For Maimonides, only a philosophical religion was a genuine religion at all; the religion of the unphilosophical masses was better than nothing, to be sure, but far from what was needed. And what is truly needed, according to Maimonides, is a path to God that is possible only through "speculative"[5] reason, the reasoning of the trained metaphysical philosopher (who was also supposed by Maimonides to have mastered mathematics and physics and astronomy!). Through pure reason this kind of philosopher is supposed to come to see that God must exist, that God must be "simple" (otherwise God would not be an absolute unity, and hence would not be perfect), that simplicity is incompatible with having a plurality of properties, and that, finally, even the notion that God exists in the same sense of "exist" that anything else does must be rejected. At this point, the philosopher is ready to grasp that God cannot be truly grasped! The "negative theology" of Maimonides was not a path to "experiential philosophy" in Rosenzweig's sense, but a path to a sort of redemptive antinomy that only the trained metaphysician is capable of appreciating, and whose appreciation is literally salvific.

Negative theology, in this medieval sense, is thus something one can discuss endlessly. But this is not what Rosenzweig, Buber, or Levinas wants us to do at all. We may have different ideas about God and about discourse con-

cerning God when we philosophize, but that sort of phi-
losophizing is not experiencing the reality of God or experiencing "the glory of the infinite," nor is it (as Maimonides
thought) a necessary propaedeutic to true religious experience. And this is something with which Wittgenstein (to
bring in the "¼" of my "3¼" Jewish philosophers for a last
time) would have certainly agreed.

In Chapter 1, I described Pierre Hadot's notion of "philosophy as a way of life." For my "3¼" Jewish philosophers,
philosophy was indeed a way of life—but only when it
leaves the page and becomes "experiential." And that is
what they wanted it to do.

Notes

INTRODUCTION (AUTOBIOGRAPHICAL)

1. My first philosophical publication, "Synonymy and the Analysis of Belief Sentences," was devoted to the question of the contribution that logical form makes to meaning; the topics of the next three were, in order, inductive logic, the philosophy of mathematics, and the logic of quantum mechanics.

2. *Renewing Philosophy* (Cambridge, Mass.: Harvard University Press, 1992) contains my Gifford Lectures, delivered at the University of St Andrews in 1990.

3. Collected in Ludwig Wittgenstein, *Lectures and Conversations on Aesthetics, Psychology and Religious Belief; Compiled from Notes Taken by Yorick Smythies, Rush Rhees and James Taylor,* edited by Cyril Barrett (Oxford: Basil Blackwell, 1966), 53–72.

4. Ibid., 148.

5. See *Ludwig Wittgenstein: Personal Recollections,* edited by Rush Rhees (Oxford: Oxford University Press, 1991), 94.

6. Gordon Kaufman, *In the Face of Mystery: A Constructive Theology* (Cambridge, Mass.: Harvard University Press, 1993).

1. ROSENZWEIG AND WITTGENSTEIN

1. From the foreword to the 1999 publication as a "Fischer Taschenbook," I learned that this notebook had long been regarded as lost. It had, in fact, been in the possession of Wittgenstein's sister, Margarete Stonborough in Gmunden, who upon Wittgenstein's death gave it to Rudolf Koder (a friend of Wittgenstein's from 1923 to his death, who shared his musical interests) and Koder's sister Elisabeth as *Erringerungsstücke* (remembrances). In 1993, Koder's son, Professor Johannes Koder (who heads the Institute for Byzantine and Modern Greek Studies at the University of Vienna), contacted the Brenner Archive of the University of Innsbruck. *Denkbewegungen; Tagebücher 1930–1932, 1936,*

1937 was first published by Heymon-Verlag, Innsbruck in 1997, and then by Fischer Taschenbuch Verlag, Frankfurt am Main, 1999.

2. The most reliable account of Wittgenstein's complicated attitude to "Jewish mentality" (a topic hotly debated in Vienna in Wittgenstein's youth) is Yuval Lurie's "Jews as a Metaphysical Species," *Philosophy* 64 (1989): 323–347.

3. An exception is the remark reported by Drury that he had "the absolutely Hebraic sense" that what we do makes a difference in the end. Maurice O'Connor Drury, "Conversations with Wittgenstein," in *Recollections of Wittgenstein,* edited by Rush Rhees (Oxford: Oxford University Press, 1984), 161.

4. In fact, Wittgenstein (who was born in 1889) and Rosenzweig (who was born in 1886) were nearly the same age. And although Rosenzweig was brought up in Germany, in Cassel, and Wittgenstein in Vienna, they exemplify a very similar purity of motivation and a remarkable quality I find difficult to describe—"intense integrity," or "integral intensity" are the closest I can come.

5. Peter Eli Gordon, *Rosenzweig and Heidegger: Between Judaism and German Philosophy* (Berkeley: University of California Press, 2003), 178.

6. That it is *profoundly* erroneous is an insight I owe to valuable conversations, extending over many years, with Stanley Cavell and James Conant.

7. Although Stanley Cavell thinks that certain "ordinary language philosophers" do hold the position that Gordon ascribes to Wittgenstein, a central thesis of Cavell's *The Claim of Reason* (Oxford: Oxford University Press, 1982), is that Wittgensteinian philosophy is profoundly opposed to the view that anyone who departs from some fixed stock of "common meanings" is automatically guilty of talking nonsense.

8. L. Wittgenstein, *Remarks on Frazer's Golden Bough,* edited by Rush Rhees (Atlantic Highlands, N.J.: Humanities Press, 1983).

9. Collected in Ludwig Wittgenstein, *Lectures and Conversations on Aesthetics, Psychology and Religious Belief; Compiled from Notes Taken by Yorick Smythies, Rush Rhees And James Taylor,* edited by Cyril Barrett (Oxford: Basil Blackwell, 1966), 53–72.

10. I discuss the nature of philosophical enlightenment(s) in my Spinoza Lectures, collected as part II of my *Ethics without Ontology* (Cambridge, Mass.: Harvard University Press, 2004).

11. Pierre Hadot, *Philosophy as a Way of Life* (Oxford: Blackwell, 1995), edited by Arnold Davidson.

12. Ibid., 265.

13. L. Wittgenstein, *Last Writings on the Philosophy of Psychology,* vol. I (Chicago: University of Chicago Press, 1982, 1990), §913.

14. *Lectures and Conversations on Aesthetics, Psychology and Religious Belief,* 53–55.

15. "The Builders" [1937], collected in Franz Rosenzweig, *On Jewish Learning* (New York: Schocken Books, 1955), edited by Nahum Glatzer, 78.

16. Abraham Geiger (1810–1874) was a founder of German Reform Judaism.

17. "The Builders," 79–80, emphasis added.

18. "On Being a Jewish Person," in *Franz Rosenzweig: His Life and Thought,* 2nd edition (New York: Schocken Books, 1953, 1962), edited by Nahum Glatzer, 222. "Liberalism" here refers to what is called Reform Judaism in the United States.

19. Franz Rosenzweig, *The Star of Redemption* (Notre Dame, Ind.: Notre Dame Press, 1985), translated from the 2nd edition of 1930 by William W. Hallo.

20. Ibid., 183.

21. The idea of seeing this formulation as expressing agreement and disagreement with Buber was suggested to me by Man Lung Cheng.

22. The original title was *Das Büchlein vom guten und kranken Menschenverstand* [The Little Book of Healthy and Sick Human Understanding]. It was written in July 1921, but not published in Rosenzweig's lifetime. In fact, its first publication was in an English translation with an introduction by Nahum Glatzer (New York: Noonday Press, 1953), under the title *Understanding the Sick and the Healthy.* It then went out of print and was reissued under the same title, with a new introduction by myself as well as the 1953 Glatzer introduction, by Harvard University Press in 1999.

23. Hans Vaihinger, *The Philosophy of "as if": A System of the Theoretical, Practical and Religious Fictions of Mankind,* translated by C. K. Ogden (London: Routledge and Kegan Paul, 1968), originally published as *Die Philosophie des "als ob," der theoretischen, praktischen und religiosen Fictionem der Menschheit auf Grund eines idealistischen Positivismus* (Berlin: Reuter and Reichard, 1911).

24. From this point on, the present chapter is taken (with minor alterations) from my "Introduction, 1999" to *Understanding the Sick and the Healthy.* Reprinted here by permission of Harvard University Press.

25. That this is the case is brilliantly argued in Charles Travis, *Unshadowed Thought* (Cambridge: Harvard University Press, 2000).

26. Derek Parfit, *Reasons and Persons* (Oxford: Oxford University Press, 1987).

27. Ibid., 49.

28. Of course, the idea of a "time-slice" *thinking* is incoherent.

Thought requires time, and requires dispositions of various kinds. Therefore the idea that all my time-slices are *selves* has only the appearance of sense. And giving the time-slices "thickness"—say, thinking of them as one-minute thick—won't help either. Ascribing dispositions to a time-slice lacks even the appearance of sense.

29. Wittgenstein famously remarked in a conversation with Drury, "I am not a religious person, but I cannot help seeing every problem from a religious point of view"(!). From *Ludwig Wittgenstein: Personal Recollections,* edited by Rush Rhees (Oxford: Oxford University Press, 1991), 94.

30. In a recently published (2006) collection of remarks by Wittgenstein's sister, Hermine, she writes in a note dated Fall 1917, "Ludwig says 'I have a conscience, I know what I myself believe to be good or bad, but I have *no religion*. I also don't know why I myself believe something to be good or bad, and I don't ask about it, because this question simply isn't in me [diese Frage nicht in mir liegt]." *"Ludwig Sagt . . ."* *Die Aufzeichnungen der Hermine Wittgenstein,* edited by Mathias Iven (Berlin: Panerga, 2006), 70.

31. Wittgenstein, *Culture and Value* (Chicago: University of Chicago Press, 1980), 64.

32. In "Non-Cognitivism and Rule-Following," reprinted in his *Mind, Value, and Reality* (Cambridge, Mass.: Harvard University Press, 1998). See p. 207.

33. See "The New Thinking" (190–208) in *Franz Rosenzweig: His Life and Thought,* 200. This section is an abridged translation by Glatzer of "Das Neue Denken," supplementary notes to *The Star of Redemption.* Rosenzweig, *Kleinere Schriften* (Berlin: Schocken Verlag, 1937), 377–398. A complete translation can be found in Franz Rosenzweig, *Philosophical and Theological Writings,* translated and edited with Notes and Commentary by Paul W. Franks and Michael Morgan (Indianapolis, Ind.: Hackett, 2000), 109–139.

34. *Franz Rosenzweig: His Life and Thought.*

35. This (quite lengthy) letter may be found in full in *Franz Rosenzweig: His Life and Thought,* 94–98.

36. An earlier book of Rosenzweig's, a scholarly study of Hegel's political philosophy.

37. Rosenzweig's German readers would have been familiar with the source of the expression *demand of the day*: Johann Wolfgang Goethe, *Spruche in Prosa* (Stuttgart: Verlag freies Geistesleben, 1999), §611, "Was aber ist deine Pflicht? Die Forderung des Tages?" [collected sayings of Goethe, first published in 1870, also published under the title *Maximen und Reflexionen*].

38. I find it astounding that Rosenzweig employs the very ter-

minology that Wittgenstein introduces when distinguishing between looking to "logic" to solve philosophical problems and conceiving of his investigation as a "grammatical" one (cf. *Philosophical Investigations,* esp. §108 and §122).

39. "The New Thinking," in *Franz Rosenzweig: His Life and Thought,* 200.

40. Ibid., 199.

41. Ibid., 201.

42. "On Being a Jewish Person," in *Franz Rosenzweig: His Life and Thought,* 222. This section, pp. 214–227 of the volume, is Nahum Glatzer's translation of a portion of *Bildung und keine Ende,* an open letter on education, *Kleinere Schriften,* 79–93.

43. I do not mean to suggest that Rosenzweig changed his mind on this aspect of his thinking, but simply that it ceased to preoccupy him.

44. "God's first word to the soul that unlocks itself to him is 'love me.'" *The Star,* 177. I shall discuss what Rosenzweig means by this in the next chapter.

2. Rosenzweig on Revelation and Romance

1. The edition I am using is Franz Rosenzweig, *The Star of Redemption* (Notre Dame, Ind: Notre Dame Press, 1985), translated from the 2nd edition of 1930 by William W. Hallo.

2. The only complete translation of "The New Thinking" in English, and the one I shall quote from in this chapter, may be found in Franz Rosenzweig, *Philosophical and Theological Writings,* translated and edited with Notes and Commentary by Paul W. Franks and Michael Morgan (Indianapolis, Ind.: Hackett, 2000), 109–139.

3. Today one might add: "and the comical attempts to 'refute' Wittgenstein's supposed theory of meaning with respect to the opening paragraphs of *Philosophical Investigations.*"

4. *Understanding the Sick and the Healthy* was not published in Rosenzweig's lifetime.

5. Latin: The end of philosophy?

6. Part III of the *Star* develops Rosenzweig's views on the special significance of just two religions, Judaism and Christianity; in the previous chapter, I expressed my lack of sympathy with those views, and I shall not discuss them in this chapter.

7. I model the term *revelatory writing* on Franks's term *revelatory speech,* which he characterizes as "language uses that assert or presuppose that the human speaker is the addressee of divine revelation." I am quoting from Paul Franks, "Revelatory Speech and Everyday Speech in Rosenzweig and Wittgenstein," *Philosophy Today* (Spring 2006): 24–39.

8. Rosenzweig, "A Note on Anthropomorphisms in Response to

the *Encyclopedia Judaica's* Article," in Rosenzweig, *God, Man, and World: Lectures and Essays,* edited and translated by Barbara E. Galli (Syracuse, N.Y.: Syracuse University Press, 1998), 138.

9. Julius Wellhausen (1844–1918) was a German biblical scholar. His "documentary hypothesis" marked the beginning of the modern understanding of the Pentateuch as a work that was not all written at one time by Moses, but rather compiled from the writings of different authors over a number of centuries.

10. This letter is collected in *Franz Rosenzweig: His Life and Thought,* 2nd edition (New York: Schocken Books, 1953, 1962), edited by Nahum Glatzer, 242–247. My quotations are from pp. 244–245.

11. Glatzer, 245.

12. Franz Rosenzweig, *The Star of Redemption* (Notre Dame, Ind.: Notre Dame Press, 1985).

13. The English translation employs the term *deictic* here, in the now rare sense of a word (like *this* or *that*) that has the function of pointing, and whose reference is determined by the context. I have replaced it with *referential.*

14. Here we see the rejection of the Hegelian doctrine of the identity of the particular and the conceptual, a rejection in which Rosenzweig follows Jacobi and Schelling.

15. Not necessarily in a temporal sense of *prior,* to be sure, but in a *logical* sense, in the German Idealist sense of *logical.*

16. *The Star of Redemption,* 227.

17. It was essential to Rosenzweig's picture that Jews should be outside of politics and not have a nation state or geographical aspirations.

18. See Peter Eli Gordon, *Rosenzweig and Heidegger: Between Judaism and German Philosophy* (Berkeley: University of California Press, 2003), for an excellent discussion of just this aspect of Rosenzweig's notion of redemption.

3. What *I and Thou* Is Really Saying

1. Yehudah Halevi (1075–1141; author of the *Kuzari*). According to Hartman, who devotes the second chapter of *Israelis and the Jewish Tradition* (New Haven, Conn.: Yale University Press, 2000) to "The God of History in Halevi," Halevi claimed that it is the history of Israel alone that "makes the divine reality accessible to human beings." (See, e.g., p. 37.)

2. Ibid., 125.

3. It was Moshe Halbertal who first pointed this out to me.

4. Martin Buber, *Ich und Du* (1923; Gerlingen: Lambert Schneider, 12th edition 1994); *I and Thou,* translated by Walter Kaufman (New

York: Scribner's Sons, 1970). The latter is the edition I cite in the present context.

5. Cf. Stanley Cavell, *Conditions Handsome and Unhandsome* (Chicago: University of Chicago Press, 1990). "Perfectionism, as I think of it, is not a competing theory of the moral life, but something like a dimension or tradition of the moral life that spans the course of Western thought, and concerns what used to be called the state of one's soul, a dimension that places tremendous burdens on personal relationships and of the transforming of oneself and of one's society" (2). In his application of this notion to Thoreau and Emerson and Wittgenstein, Cavell discerns other aspects of perfectionism than the ones I mention here— aspects having to do with the "ordinary" or the "common," both as what we are alienated from, and as what we need to transform. (This concern is foreshadowed in his *The Senses of Walden*.)

6. Levinas, "Martin Buber and the Theory of Knowledge," in *The Philosophy of Martin Buber* (LaSalle, Ill.: Open Court, The Library of Living Philosophers, 1967).

7. According to a famous story in the Talmud (BT Shabbat 31a), a heathen once came to Hillel and asked him to teach him the Talmud while he stood on one foot. Hillel answered "What is hateful to you do not do to your neighbor. That is the whole Torah. The rest is commentary; go and learn it."

8. *I and Thou*, 117–119.

9. *I and Thou*, 149 and 159, for example.

10. G. E. Moore, *Principia Ethica* (Cambridge: Cambridge University Press, revised edition 1993), first published 1903.

11. John Maynard Keynes, *Essays and Sketches in Biography* (New York: Meridian Books, 1956); originally published in *Essays in Biography* (London: Macmillan, 1933 and many other editions).

12. These efforts at "mensuration" are gently mocked by Keynes (*Essays and Sketches in Biography*, 244–246). However, Keynes also writes, "It seems to me looking back that this religion of ours was a very good one to grow up under. It remains nearer the truth than any other I know, with less extraneous matter and nothing to be ashamed of; though it is a comfort today to be able to discard with a good conscience the calculus and the mensuration and the duty to know *exactly* what one means and feels. It was a purer, sweeter air by far than Freud cum Marx. It is still my religion under the surface" (Ibid., 248).

4. Levinas on What Is Demanded of Us

1. In "A Religion for Adults," in *Difficult Freedom: Essays on Judaism,* translated by Seán Hand (London: Athlone, 1990), Levinas speaks of "my feelings in a Stalag in Germany when, over the grave of a Jewish

comrade *whom the Nazis had wanted to bury like a dog,* a Catholic priest, Father Chesnet, recited prayers which were, in the absolute sense of the term Semitic" (12). I have added emphasis to call attention to the sort of captors Levinas had (not "German soldiers" but "Nazis") and to the attitude of these captors to their Jewish prisoners of war.

2. Cf. "Ethics as First Philosophy," in *The Levinas Reader* (75–87).

3. This is the gravamen of Levinas's most famous work, *Totalité et infini* (The Hague: Martinus Nijhoff, 1961), trans. as *Totality and Infinity* by Alphonso Lingis (same publisher, 1969); (Pittsburgh: Duquesne University Press, 1969, 1979).

4. This is a major theme in *Totality and Infinity.*

5. This is a theme that has also been sounded in Anglo-American philosophy, e.g., by pragmatists and also by Thomas Nagel in *The View from Nowhere* (Oxford: Oxford University Press, 1986).

6. Levinas, *Ethics and Infinity; Conversations with Philippe Nemo,* translated by R. A. Cohen (Pittsburgh: Duquesne University Press, 1985), 75–76.

7. Cf. Stanley Cavell, *Conditions Handsome and Unhandsome* (Chicago: University of Chicago Press, 1990). "Perfectionism, as I think of it, is not a competing theory of the moral life, but something like a dimension or tradition of the moral life that spans the course of Western thought, and concerns what used to be called the state of one's soul, a dimension that places tremendous burdens on personal relationships and of the transforming of oneself and of one's society" (2).

8. As the examples of Kant and Mill illustrate, the fact that a philosopher is a Cavellian "perfectionist" need not preclude his also making a "legislative" contribution.

9. "The ego . . . is reduced to the 'here I am' [*me voici*], in a transparency without opaqueness, without heavy zones propitious for evasion. 'Here I am' as a witness of the Infinite, but a witness that does not thematize what it bears witness of, and whose truth is not the truth of representation, is not evidence." *Otherwise than Being or Beyond Essence,* translated by Alphonso Lingis (Dordrecht: Kluwer, 1991), 146 [cited henceforth as *Otherwise than Being*]. In a note to this paragraph (n. 11), Levinas cites Isaiah, writing, "'Here I am! send me." Isaiah, 6:8. Here I am!' means 'send me'." Note that "send me" is not a proposition.

10. Cf. "Love and Filiation," in *Ethics and Infinity,* 63–72.

11. *Time and the Other,* translated by Richard Cohen (Pittsburgh: Duquesne University Press, 1987). Of course, fully appreciating the relation with the other requires fully appreciating the *mortality* of the other; the contrast with Heidegger could not be more complete.

12. *Otherwise than Being,* 46.

13. Ephraim Meir has remarked (in a private communication)

that this also presents me as one who hears the basic commandment "Thou shalt not kill," and that in Levinas's philosophy this basic commandment is also a Saying. Levinas deconstructs the commandment as a "said" in order to point to the Saying.

14. *Der Logische Aufbau der Welt*, 4th edition (Hamburg: Felix Meiner, 1974), Section 64, p.86.

15. Edmund Husserl, *Ideas: General Introduction to Pure Phenomenology*, translated by W. R. Boyce Gibson (New York: Collier, 1962, first published in English in 1931; the first volume of *Ideen* dates back to 1913).

16. I am indebted to Abe Stone for convincing me of the extent of Husserl's influence on Carnap, up to and including the period of the *Aufbau*. Stone observed that even the expression "Aufbau der Welt" occurs in Husserl [vol. VII of the *Husserliana* volumes, 175, ll. 33–34].

17. Abe Stone reminds me that Carnap did not want to simply use mathematical logic to reproduce Husserl's system constitution, but to get it out of exactly this problem. "In particular, he wants to replace alleged metaphysical truths, including those that have to do with metaphysical *priority*, with (conventional) truths about language. (Hence he approvingly quotes Nietzsche as saying that the 'ego' is an artifact of our language, resulting from the fact that every sentence must have a subject" (personal communication from Stone). Stone is right, but the fact remains that the "primitive experiences" [*Urerlebnisse*] of Carnap's system are what we in ordinary language call *my* experiences, and not the experiences of human beings in general. (For a discussion of Carnap's failure to successfully avoid solipsism, see my "Logical Positivism and Intentionality," collected in my *Words and Life* [Cambridge, Mass.: Harvard University Press, 1994], 85–98.) This is one of the reasons that Levinas would not have been satisfied with Carnap's attempt any more than he was satisfied with Husserl's.

18. *Otherwise than Being*, 78.

19. Ibid., 78; explanations in square brackets are mine.

20. I am indebted once again to Abe Stone for pointing out the significance of Levinas's discussions of Descartes's proof (e.g., *Ethics and Infinity*, 91–92; *Otherwise than Being or Beyond Essence*, 146; *The Levinas Reader*, 112, 173–175). Stone writes (in a personal communication), "What needs noticing, I think (as much for the proper understanding of Descartes as for the proper understanding of Levinas) is the moment at the end of the First Meditation where Descartes speaks of being like a prisoner who awakens in a dark prison. Levinas notes that this represents a stage *before* the cogito argument."

21. In a different reference to this argument from the one given in the previous note, Levinas writes: "[Knowledge] is by essence a re-

lation with what one equals and includes, with that whose alterity one suspends, with what becomes immanent, because it is to my measure and to my scale. I think of Descartes, who said that the *cogito* can give itself the sun and the sky; the only thing it cannot give itself is the idea of the Infinite" (*Ethics and Infinity*, 60). Here Levinas is in the midst of answering a series of questions on his own discussion not of God but of the relation to other people in the lectures published as *Time and the Other.*

22. "The concept of the infinite," Kant says, "is taken from mathematics and belongs only to it." And although "I might call the divine understanding 'infinite' . . . this does not help me in the least to be able to say determinately how great the divine understanding is. Thus we see that I cannot come a single step further in my cognition of God by applying the concept of mathematical infinity to Him." The quotation is from pp. 361–362 (AK XXVIII, 1017, 1018) of the "Lectures on the Philosophical Doctrine of Religion," collected in *The Cambridge Edition of the Works of Immanuel Kant: Religion and Rational Theology*, translated and edited by Allen Wood and George Di Giovanni (Cambridge: Cambridge University Press, 1996), 345–451, delivered in the 1870s after the first critique was published. I am grateful to Carl Posy for helping me track down this passage.

23. *Ethics and Infinity*, 57.

24. See Chapter V, section 2, "The Glory of the Infinite" in *Otherwise than Being*, 140–162.

25. "The Pact" in *The Levinas Reader*, 225–226.

26. *Otherwise than Being or Beyond Essence*, 89.

27. I see the idea of "interrupting" being's "unrendable essence" as reflecting the idea we encountered in Levinas's reading of Descartes's proof, the idea that the other breaks all my categories, like a "fissure of being."

28. *Otherwise than Being or Beyond Essence*, 90.

29. In Levinas's footnote at this point, the notion of "obsession"— a Levinasian term for the recognition of the other as obligating me, the ethical relation par excellence—is connected with "infinity" and also with going beyond "intentionality," i.e., once again with going beyond the metaphysical categories.

30. In this case the attribute that "Thou shalt not see my face; for no man can see me and live" [Exod. 33:20].

31. Two sentences later, Levinas writes that "life is still not arrested in the absolute immobility of a death mask. The ending up of finitude is not an appearance, which Hegel was able to designate as 'a being which *immediately* is its own nothingness.'"

32. *Ethics and Infinity*, 88–89.

33. Places in Lithuania—Vilna and Kovno in particular—were the great centers of Ashkenazi Jewish learning. The Lithuanian Jews were famous for their insistence on rigorous argument and for their contempt for the enthusiastic and charismatic religiosity associated with Hasidism. Levinas himself was born in Kovno.

34. Collected in *Difficult Freedom*, 11–23.

35. Collected in *Difficult Freedom*, 273–276 (quotation is from p. 275).

36. E.g., it isn't true that there are no "charismatic" streams in Judaism. (Think of Hasidism, of various strains of Messianism). However, it must be admitted that when Judaism is referred to, most often it is the austere variety that is meant; Hasidism is regularly marginalized, with Buber and Heschel being the great exceptions to this rule.

37. *A Heart of Many Rooms: Celebrating the Many Voices within Judaism* (Woodstock, Vt.: Jewish Lights Publishing, 1999).

38. Exod. 23:2, which the rabbis took out of context to justify the principle that the Jewish law is decided by majority vote of the great scholars.

39. On this, see *A Living Covenant: The Innovative Spirit in Traditional Judaism* (Woodstock, Vt: Jewish Lights Publishing, 1997) by David Hartman, and *Rational Rabbis* (Bloomington: Indiana University Press, 1997), by Menahem Fisch.

40. BT (Babylonian Talmud), *Pirqei Avot*, I:12.

41. BT *Shabbat* 31a.

42. The reference to the Liberation shows that it is French Jews who are here addressed, but what Levinas goes on to say clearly concerns all Jews who live in modern times.

43. "Judaism and the Present," 252–259 in *The Levinas Reader* (quotation is from p. 255).

44. Ibid., 255–256.

45. All the quotations in this paragraph are from p. 256.

46. Ibid., 256.

47. Ibid., 256–257. As Ephraim Meir pointed out to me, it is because Levinas makes Judaism's function an *ethical* one that it must stand outside the dialectic; there needs to be a standpoint from which historical "development" can itself be *criticized*, and that standpoint is the ethical standpoint. But Levinas is not naïve; the ethical standpoint is not a set of timeless principles and codes, but something more basic than all principles and codes. Concerning the relation between ethics and politics, see "Paix et proximité," in *Emmanuel Levinas, Les Cahiers de la nuit surveillée* 23 (Lagrasse: Editions Verdier, 1984), 339–346, and see already "Liberté et commandement," *Revue de metaphysiqe et de morale* (1953), reprinted in E. Levinas, *Liberté et commandement* (Paris: Fata

Morgana: 1994), 27–53. On this subject see also Ephraim Meir, "mil-hama v'shalom behagut shel levinas" *Iyyun* 48 (1997): 471–479.

48. Compare Rosenzweig's claim that Judaism is an ahistoric religion, which we mentioned in chapter 1.

49. *The Levinas Reader*, 258.

50. BT *Kiddushin* 40b.

51. *The Levinas Reader*, 257.

52. Ibid., 257

53. "No theme, no present, has a capacity for the Infinite," in *Otherwise than Being*, 146.

54. "Martin Buber and the Theory of Knowledge," in *The Levinas Reader*, 70.

55. Here Levinas uses the word *evidence* in the sense of a presence or a disclosure, not in the sense of "evidence for a hypothesis."

56. In the next paragraph Levinas connects this idea of an "exception to the rule of being" with Descartes's proof that we discussed above: "The idea of the Infinite, which in Descartes is lodged in a thought that cannot contain it, expresses the disproportion between glory and the present" (146).

57. *Otherwise than Being*, 146.

58. *Ethics and Infinity*, 105.

59. Chapter VIII, "Responsibility for the Other," in *Ethics and Infinity*, 99–100.

60. Levinas means that the true life (human life in the normative sense of human) is absent if one rests with being "scandalized." The passage continues: "The humanity in historical and objective being, the very breakthrough of the subjective, of the human psychism in its original vigilance or sobering up, is being which undoes its condition of being: dis-*interestedness*."

61. *Otherwise than Being*, 128.

62. A criticism of Levinasian ethics that I heard voiced by Milllie Heyd in a wonderful dinner conversation.

AFTERWORD

1. "Atheistic Theology" is the title of one of the essays collected in Franz Rosenzweig, *Philosophical and Theological Writings*, translated and edited with Notes and Commentary by Paul W. Franks and Michael Morgan (Indianapolis, Ind.: Hackett, 2000), 10–24.

2. I am on Buber's side here; "total responsibility" for the other seems to me to go beyond what it is right to demand. Levinas enthusiasts will of course accuse me of "chickening out" here.

3. "The New Thinking" is collected in Franz Rosenzweig, *Philosophical and Theological Writings*, 109–139.

4. Latin: "the end of philosophy."

5. "Speculative" reason, in its ancient sense, was reason that perceived ("saw") metaphysical truths. The appearance of the present usage of "speculate," to mean "engage in reasoning about what *might* be the case," reflects post-Enlightenment distrust of the claims of metaphysics to apodictic certainty.

Hilary Putnam

Born in Chicago and educated at the University of Pennsylvania, Harvard University, and the University of California at Los Angeles, Hilary Putnam taught at Northwestern University, Princeton University, and the Massachusetts Institute of Technology before moving to Harvard University in 1965. In his early years at Harvard, he was an outspoken opponent of the war in Vietnam. Although he writes in the idiom of analytic philosophy, Putnam addresses major themes relating science to ethics. He also taught Jewish philosophy at Harvard in the decade before his retirement in 2000. His many books include *Ethics without Ontology; The Threefold Cord: Mind, Body, and World; Words and Life;* and *Pragmatism: An Open Question.* He is a past president of the American Philosophical Association (Eastern Division), the Philosophy of Science Association, and the Association for Symbolic Logic.